WRITING YOUR DISSERTATION

How To Books for Students

Backpacking Round Europe
Budgeting for Students
Critical Thinking for Students
Gaining a Master's Degree
Getting a Job after University
Getting a Place at University
Going to University
How to Know Your Rights: Students
How to Know Your Rights: Teachers
How to Master Book-Keeping
How to Master GCSE Accounts
How to Master Languages
How to Start Word Processing
How to Study Abroad
How to Study & Learn
How to Study & Live in Britain
How to Survive at College
How to Teach Abroad
How to Use a Library
Mastering Business English
Passing Exams Without Anxiety
Passing That Interview
Planning Your Gap Year
Research Methods
Spending a Year Abroad
Studying at University
Studying for a Degree
Taking Your A-Levels
Writing an Assignment
Writing an Essay
Writing a Report
Writing Business Letters
Writing Your Dissertation

Other titles in preparation

The How To series now contains more than 200 titles in the following categories:

Business Management
Computer Basics
General Reference
Jobs & Careers
Living & Working Abroad
Personal Finance
Self-Development
Small Business
Student Handbooks
Successful Writing

Please send for a free copy of the latest catalogue for full details (see back cover for address).

WRITING YOUR DISSERTATION

How to plan, prepare and present your work successfully

Derek Swetnam

2nd edition

How To Books

Cartoons by Mike Flanagan

British Library Cataloguing-in-Publication data
A catalogue record for this book is available from the British Library.

Published by How To Books Ltd, 3 Newtec Place, Magdalen Road, Oxford OX4 1RE, United Kingdom.
Tel: (01865) 793806. Fax: (01865) 248780.

First edition 1995
Second edition 1997
Third impression 1997
Fourth impression 1998

Note: The material contained in this book is set out in good faith for general guidance and no liability can be accepted for loss or expense incurred as a result of relying in particular circumstances on statements made in the book. The laws and regulations are complex and liable to change, and readers should check the current position with the relevant authorities before making personal arrangements.

Produced for How To Books by Deer Park Productions.
Typeset by Kestrel Data, Exeter.
Printed and bound in Great Britain by The Cromwell Press, Trowbridge, Wiltshire.

Contents

List of Illustrations

Preface

to the Second Edition

Almost every higher education course in the country requires a thesis, dissertation or research project of some considerable length in full or partial fulfilment of its qualification. Such an undertaking often strikes terror into the average student, who is typically assumed to be able to work alone, to understand all the principles of research and to have high-level reading and writing skills. Where these have been acquired is not always apparent.

Some institutions offer excellent research methods courses and impeccable support; others, sadly, leave students to sink in a sea of panic which leads to high rates of non-completion or drop-out.

There are many top grade books on research methods but most assume that the researcher is a professional with unlimited time and resources. This book is based on the real experiences of students who do not match such a description but who need ideas for planning and producing a good piece of work without stress and total disruption of their personal life.

The basics are: asking a question, finding the answer and reporting the answer. It sounds easy: it can be easy and enjoyable but only for the organised and committed student.

For this second edition, some sections have been revised and extended with more, actual examples. However, the aim remains: to help you, the reader, to build confidence through practical planning and developing brief, realistic strategies for success in writing your dissertation.

Derek Swetnam

IS THIS YOU?

Undergraduate

Research student

Master's student

Nursing student

Studying education

Market researcher

OU student

Mature student

Part-time student

Teacher

Student supervisor

Lecturer

Doing a project

Report writer

Returning to study

Caring professional

Postgraduate

Industrial researcher

Improving writing skills

Foreign student

Social worker

Studying science/technology

Planning research

Distance learner

Revising rusty techniques

Social scientist

Preparing for a higher degree

1
Before You Start

CHECKING THE REQUIREMENTS

Congratulations! You have been accepted for a higher-level course or have reached the stage where a taught course moves into the dissertation, project or extended study phase. There are over 5,000 postgraduate courses alone offered by universities and colleges in Great Britain and countless other courses demanding at some stage a potentially daunting individual research study.

Research is inquiry into some aspect of the physical, natural or social world. It must be systematic, critical, empirical and have academic integrity. All students should assume that their work will be subject to public scrutiny and whatever approach is used readers must be convinced that all the recommendations and conclusions are firmly grounded in meticulous work.

You would certainly not have been admitted to your course if the staff did not think that you could pass. The greatest danger is not failure but non-submission and some courses which appear to have high failure rates in fact reflect the latter.

This book is about planning, strategy and keeping your sanity while producing a good class piece of work.

Although every educational organisation has its own idiosyncratic requirements they have many features in common and general principles apply to all. Apart from the very best PhD work all student research is a compromise between what is desirable and what is possible. Mature, part-time students will need to keep a fine balance between the demands of job, family and course.

Mature students have special problems which they are often very reluctant to share. They have a high ego stake in the qualification, especially if they are already in a senior post. There may be other more junior members of staff who have already achieved the qualification. They often feel that their academic writing skills have atrophied and that they will be overwhelmed by the phenomenal brain power of the other students. Almost by definition the older student is more prone to marital, family and health problems.

Few of these fears are ever realised and are usually more than compensated for by the wisdom and motivation that comes with age. Whatever problems you may have it is certain that someone else has experienced and overcome them. Beware of rationalising difficulties: that is blaming home, job, health and family unfairly for your lack of progress. Confide in your supervisor and most will move heaven and earth to assist.

Assessing your abilities

If your course is optional and especially part-time you will almost certainly have terrible butterflies in the stomach about your ability to see it through. This is absolutely normal. Try the following self-assessment:

1. Do you have the motivation and commitment?
2. Can you cope with the demands of your job and family as well?
3. Do you have the reading and writing skills?
4. Can you face the travelling and possible evening work?
5. Can you afford the course fees or obtain funding?
6. Can you work on your own?
7. Do you respond to pressure and deadlines?

If that all seems a bit gloomy try this:

1. Are you looking for an exciting and rewarding experience?
2. Do you want to expand your thinking powers?
3. Do you want to meet stimulating people?
4. Are you ready to enhance your career opportunities?
5. Do you want to feel proud of your achievement?

Convinced? Here is a tip from one of my students who had every possible personal problem during her research. **Do not associate your dissertation too closely with your work or professional life**. Regard it as an escape from stress, not as an addition to it; it really helps.

Building your confidence

A great preventer of progress is lack of confidence and the insecurity that results. To start your confidence-building programme check all the details of the requirements and regulations as follows:

- What is the exact date of submission?
- What wordage is required?
- Are there any intermediate specified dates, eg literature review completed by?
- How must the work be presented?
- What are the rules about format?
- What tutorial support is available?

It is quite helpful to see actual examples of previous student work, available from the department or library, if only to convince you that you can do better than many of those that were accepted!

It is strongly advised that the house style and format is adopted from the outset (see Chapter 6). Even if the student is a computer expert, re-formatting many pages of text, especially if desperate for time, can be a frustrating task.

The wordage in research projects varies from about 10,000 up to 60,000 or more for a high-level pure research degree, the average at master's level being 25,000. There has been a distinct tendency in recent years for these figures to be reduced. If the numbers produce a sick feeling in the stomach be reassured that exceeding the limit is a far more common problem than the reverse.

The crucial issue of using tutors will be returned to later.

CHOOSING A SUBJECT

This apparently simple process can be agony. Usually only general parameters are given, yet great precision is expected. You will be seriously handicapped unless the topic is one in which you are interested enough to spend up to a year or more and to sustain that interest during hours of work. The dissertation should be 'about something': the days when rambling, discursive essays were accepted have long gone and you must never start without a detailed plan, preferably also a title even though this may be subsequently modified.

The selection process

The process is rather like sharpening a pencil, for example:

- General area of study—sociology
- Particular interest—groups of old people
- More specifically—community care
- Especially—in residential homes
- Precisely—in warden-controlled homes
- Draft title—'The management of community care in warden-controlled residential homes'.

The eventual fine point is the working title which may be further refined or limited to one exact location. From this stage another useful technique is to develop an ideas list which covers about 30 possibilities for the research, to be edited down as the research questions are developed. Some students do a personal brainstorm or draw multilegged spiders with an idea on each leg. If you have access to others on the course that is a useful stage at which to exchange views with them and/or arrange an initial tutorial meeting.

CHECKING FEASIBILITY

The title and the ideas may sound wonderful but are they possible? However worthy it may be to survey 50 local authorities, can you support the postage, cost and travel that such a project implies? One undergraduate proposed researching the roles of Thomas Hardy and Arnold Bennett as regional novelists in six months: at least 15 novels to be read!

It is more important for you to achieve the qualification and stay sane than to impress the academic world with an amazing work of erudition. If appropriate, high-level scholarship may be developed later from the work in hand.

Many of the ideas on the first list will have to be crossed out on the grounds of impracticability. Check the following:

- Is the project physically possible in time, distance and volume of work?
- Can it be afforded? (50 letters plus SAEs cost around £20.)
- Do you have, or can you develop rapidly, the skills needed for the research?
- Will you be permitted to gain access to the suggested sites?
- Can you find the necessary literature?
- Are there any ethical or moral problems?
- Will the topic remain 'live' over the period of the research?
- Would you have the support of the college and/or your employer?

Do not assume anything. If in doubt about access get written confirmation. A burning issue in schools or the health service can be extinguished by legislation. Many education students working in the mid-1980s had their research shot to pieces by the 1988 Education Act.

Be particularly careful if you plan to research with children or ethnic minorities. While most employers are helpful and co-operative some can be jealous or obstructive, especially if the work may reveal defects in an existing system.

WATCHING ETHICAL PRACTICE

Students may be surprised when they are given a written policy on the ethics of research and even asked to sign that they have read it. Some of these can be quite complex, especially where physical research on people or animals is involved, but all students should follow some general principles which are common to all policies. You have a duty to ensure that:

- no harm should come to participants in the research either physically, mentally or socially
- particular care is taken not to exploit the vulnerability of children, the elderly, the disabled or those disadvantaged in any way
- no physical or environmental damage should be caused
- wherever possible participants are informed of the nature of the work and give their consent
- the research follows equal opportunities principles
- anonymity and privacy, where requested, are guaranteed and honoured
- nothing is done that brings your institution into disrepute.

PLANNING REALISTIC TIME SCALES

Remember that you do not really have all the time that your institution has apparently allocated for submission. One must think positively but here are some factors that regularly cause the operation of 'Murphy's Law' which states that if anything can go wrong, it will!

- family problems
- illness
- holidays (yes, they are needed)
- computer failures
- contacting tutors
- rejection of manuscript
- delays in typing and binding.

If none of these occurs you have a bonus!

Don't be pessimistic but be realistic. Students who are unable to use a word processor may find difficulties in employing a typist (50 pence a page or more) and three weeks may be required. Professional binding can take from two days to two weeks.

A dissertation which is to be completed 'in a year' must actually be done in nine months and most students find that procrastination can easily become a way of life. A general guide for any extended project or research is to plan to use only 75% of the supposed time available, which should be tentatively allocated as follows:

Introduction	5%
Literature review	35%
Research methods	10%
Data collection	20%
Analysis	15%
Conclusions and recommendations	10%
Bibliography and appendices	5%

This general balance holds good for a wide range of research types. However, scientific and experimental work may have the data collection part extended, particularly in higher degrees. The boundaries are not discrete and the reading and updating of literature runs throughout.

PRODUCING YOUR MASTER PLAN

The choice of general area of study is easy as it is usually defined for us by circumstances, our abilities and the course that has been undertaken. It is the refinement, focusing and development of the research questions that present a hurdle. Take a deep breath and answer these three questions:

- What do you want to know?
- How are you going to find out?
- What will you do with the answers?

From an amorphous, vague idea must emerge a sharp, precise **plan**. The initial notion will be modified by contact with colleagues, reading and practical considerations which will provide you with a location in your own work area or outside it. The purpose of the work should become clear: is it to develop theory, to monitor practice, to evaluate, to increase understanding, to recommend policy?

From this process are produced several research questions and possibly **a hypothesis**. The latter is a premise based on observation or known facts that provides a basis for empirical testing to prove or disprove it. While this may be essential in pure scientific research it is often inappropriate in education or social sciences where hypotheses can emerge as the work proceeds. However, there is no escape in any area from defining the problem or questions.

You may be directed to propose a hypothesis. It is usually central to experimental research although many great scientific discoveries have been made without one! In the social sciences an over punctilious insistence on hypotheses often leads to absurdity or verbal gymnastics to explain why the original hypothesis was completely superseded. Based on the definition above which of the following are valid hypotheses?

1. Hybrid animals within a species live longer than pure bred ones.

2. Boys who play the flute and girls who play the drums are more likely to be bullied at school than children who take up instruments considered 'more appropriate' to their gender.

3. Prisoners should not be kept more than two to a cell.

4. Intrapartum asphyxia is a major cause of cerebral palsy.

5. St Lucy's High School needs a marketing policy.

6. Open-cast mining has detrimental social and economic effects on the immediately surrounding area.

Are there any that might have *emerged* from research?

Answering the question, 'How are you going to find out?' demands some knowledge of basic research styles. Positivist work is concerned only with observable, objective facts: interpretative or subjective work uses explanation and interpretation. Associated terms are **quantitative**: numbers and measuring, and **qualitative**: qualities, description and appearance. Although some researchers take an inflexible stance on these, in practice much valuable work has areas of overlap. Note at this stage that a study of research methods will be required as well as the general reading.

This may all sound very onerous and so far not a word has been written! It is nothing to the tangle that will result if planning is skimped. The master plan will show what is to be done, why? where? and in what time?

CHECKLIST

Have you:

- checked and understood the general requirements?
- chosen, refined and focused your subject?
- examined its feasibility?
- selected a tentative title?
- suggested a time scale?
- proposed a location?
- discussed ideas with peers and tutors?

CASE STUDIES

Paul chooses a subject close to home

Paul is in his final year of a BA Geography course at university. His prime interest is in human geography and his research project of 10,000 words must be done in the final year while still completing taught elements of the course. The university allows only three blank weeks for data collection. His initial suggestion of 'a look at out-of-town shopping' seems hopelessly difficult and likely to need extensive travel, but a chance remark by a colleague reminds him of the furore caused in his home town by open-cast mining: a familiar area, some knowledge—that's it! A brainstorm produces ten ideas and a possible title: 'A study of the social and economic effects of open-cast mining'.

Alison's topic is work-related

Alison is the deputy head of a Roman Catholic, inner-city secondary school. Despite the heavy demands of the job and having two small children she has completed two part-time taught years of an MA in Educational Studies. A 20,000-word dissertation must now be completed in one academic year as she was unable to produce anything last year owing to family pressures. The general parameters given are: curriculum, special education or management. She is advised by a tutor to 'focus on something accessible' and decides to make an ideas list on the management of her own school.

2
What is Involved?

JUDGING HOW MUCH WORK

It is possible for an able student to write 2,000 words in a morning, but most such attempts end in disaster. All initial writing should be considered as draft and the student must not develop an over fondness for any part. Whole areas may have to be revised or ruthlessly edited out as the work develops. Although the dissertation is original it has to contain many references to the work of others, quotations and perhaps diagrams or tables. One difficult page may take an hour.

You should try to do some work **every week**; even a few minutes is important as it helps to maintain motivation and a sense of overall purpose and shape. If this is lost the work can easily degenerate into a series of disjointed essays.

Some students find that a disciplined time-table is useful, others find that too restrictive, but whichever style you adopt regular production is essential.

Depending on the level, you have between ten and twenty major aspects to address including the focusing that has already been done. The research questions can be further refined and should be constantly referred to before each new area of work. Reading and recording the literature and research methods literature may be a third of the task.

PLANNING YOUR TASKS

It is not intended that the task plan, Figure 1, be slavishly adhered to—individual circumstances vary. For example, some institutions strictly limit the students' choices. However, all successful students follow the basic strategies.

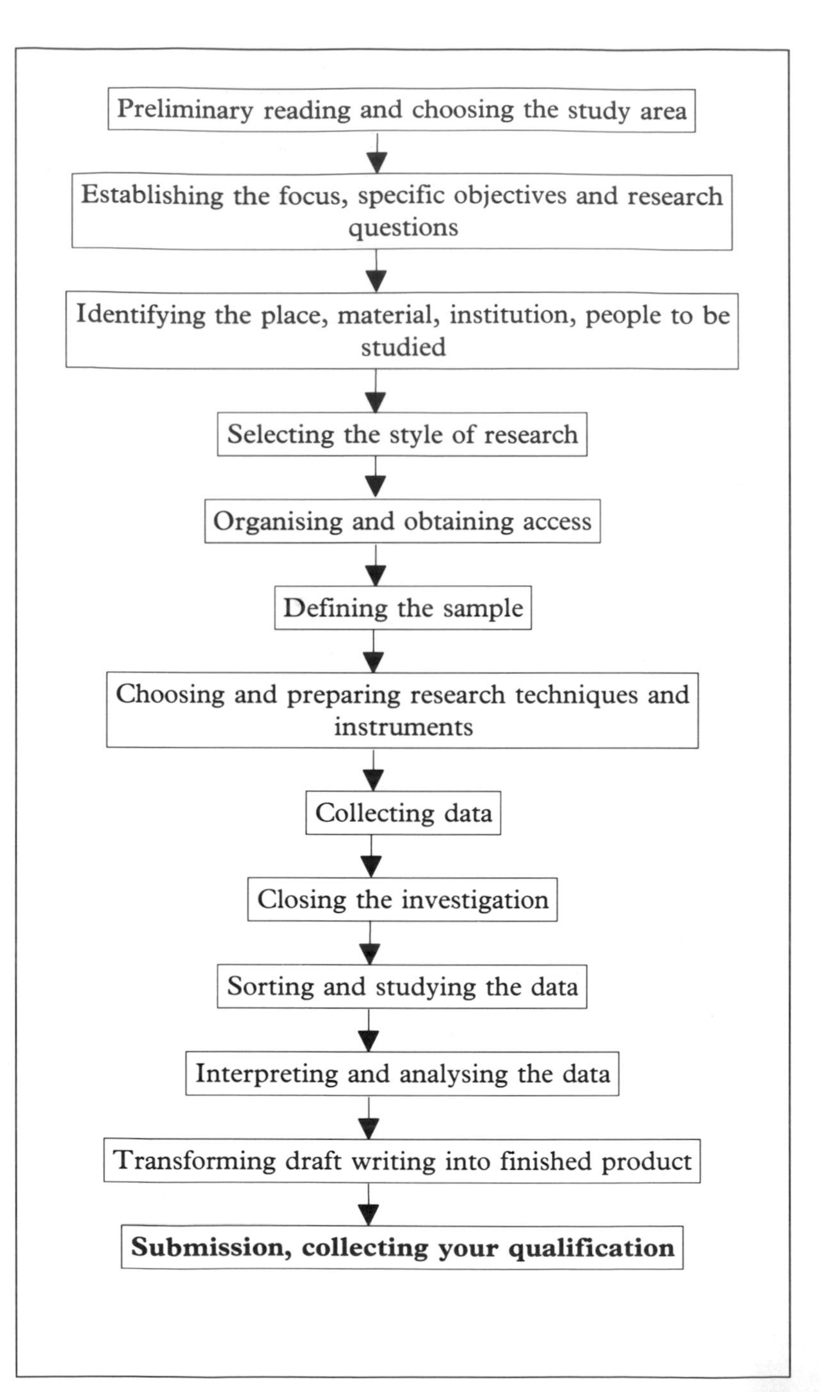

Fig. 1. A typical task plan.

See if you can match some of the stages of the flow chart in Figure 1 with the following narrative:

> A nursing student has read three general texts about the relative effects of different types of care on newly born babies. The texts indicate that this area has been researched extensively by both amateurs and professionals but still interests him greatly.
>
> The student, in discussion with a tutor, focuses the proposed work more narrowly on premature baby care in home and hospital. The research is to evaluate the present system and to discover the differences between home and hospital-based care, making recommendations.
>
> The study will be based on Ward 27, Hightown General Hospital in association with the two senior nurses responsible.
>
> The work will be a case study of the Post Natal group of Ward 27 and careful negotiation will be required to obtain admission to sensitive areas. Close attachment to one nurse tutor is suggested.
>
> Circumstances dictate an opportunity sample of up to five mothers and babies in each type of care, and observation and interviews will be used to collect data over a six-week period defined by the department.

As well as helping with planning, the task plan may serve vital functions such as clarifying thinking, refining and focusing, and judging the balance between desirability and feasibility mentioned in Chapter 1.

Despite the apparently restricted scope of the above study, some fairly high-level skills and knowledge will be required. Even at stage 2 warning bells may be ringing about such issues as access, ethics and academic levels. It is better to make a short trip back to the drawing board at stage 1 or 2 than a stressful journey after several weeks.

How far do Paul and Alison (the characters in our Case Studies) follow the Figure 1 Task Plan?

WRITING, REVISING AND EDITING

A question often asked is whether the dissertation should be written up as the research proceeds or at the end. While there are

DISSERTATION PROPOSAL

Draft title

An evaluation of community facilities at Hightown Leisure Centre: their use, management and development.

Aim of the research

Following recent criticisms from organisations and the public that the use of the new leisure centre is restricted to certain groups, the study aims to investigate the present use of the centre and to determine whether some people are disadvantaged by the facilities currently offered.

The study will concentrate particularly on the use made of the centre by mothers of small children, ethnic minority groups and the elderly over a six-month period. The hypothesis is that greater community use would result if more attention was paid to the needs of these groups. It is intended that the research will result in practical management recommendations.

Questions to be addressed include:

1. Are there perceived and real inadequacies in provision?
2. Do they disadvantage certain social groups?
3. Does this have an undesirable effect on community relations?
4. How may provision be made more equitable?

Style and techniques

The work will be a case study generalisable to other similar centres. Use will also be made of survey and documentary analysis. Instruments for data collection will principally be interview and questionnaire to obtain descriptive statistics.

Theoretical base and initial reading

Reference will be made to management theory, management of change and multicultural education.

Lovett (1982) *Adult education, community development and the working class.*

Cahill (1986) Community education and adult education: contrasting needs of participants and non-participants. *Journal of Community Education.*

Field (1991) Post 16, community education and racial equality. *Multicultural Teaching.*

Fig. 2. A sample dissertation proposal.

undoubtedly people who can make sense of piles of notes and cope with hours of writing, most cannot. It is also very reassuring to see whole completed sections, subject always to revisions and amendments as the work develops.

You are strongly advised to write up as soon as the material is ready. There will be many occasions when you will re-read each chapter or come across new and valuable additions to your stock. Unorganised material gets into an even greater tangle when tinkered with, whereas a good typed copy can be marked with a pen and easily seen. Resist the temptation to edit at odd times: keep an edit list with the page number of each edit, omission or error and tackle each chapter systematically.

DEVISING A SCHEDULE

You may be required by your institution to provide a **schedule** or proposal either devised by yourself or according to their format. In either case and to assist your own thinking, the following outline should be useful:

- What are the theme, purpose and main objectives of the research?
- Where will it take place?
- What is the hypothesis (for scientific research)?
- What is the theoretical basis of the research? (You may need tutorial advice for this.)
- What general, preliminary reading has given you ideas?
- What might the research lead to or be useful for?

At higher levels, such as MPhil or PhD, greater complexity will be required and you may have to present your submission to a committee.

The great enemy here is vagueness. Avoid words like 'have a look at', 'try to' and 'see if'; be **positive** and examine, measure, evaluate, survey and assess.

For an example see Figure 2.

Other headings that you may come across include: anticipated problems, equipment, ethical dimensions and costing.

KEEPING A SENSE OF PROPORTION

Reference has already been made to checking the precise requirements for the project. It is also essential to know the proportion of **marks** that is awarded to the dissertation within the total qualification. Variations may be between 10% and 100%. Even in a taught master's degree the thesis mark may be only one-third of the total; however, inevitably, passing this section is a condition of obtaining the degree.

This knowledge should help you to allocate time to complete the thesis without losing your friends, family and sanity! It is not a great idea to end up with both your qualification and a divorce.

It is important to get the co-operation of those near to you at college or at home so that if you allocate a particular evening or Saturday morning to the project, it is inviolable.

Experience shows that most successful students distribute their workload in the following pattern over 12 months (pro rata for shorter times):

- Reading, note-making, planning, setting up systems, writing the introduction: three months.
- Writing the literature review: two months.
- Refining and writing up the research methodology: one month.
- Carrying out and recording empirical work: one month.
- Analysing data: one month.
- Preparing conclusions and recommendations, appendices, bibliography, final amendments: one month.
- Proofreading, corrections, binding: one month.

You will find that the remaining two months mysteriously disappear.

ASSESSING YOUR OWN PROPOSALS

Be able at any time to answer the questions 'What is this research for? What is its value? What will it add to theory or practice in the real world?' If you are unable to do so, the focusing suggested in Chapter 1 has not been carried out properly and this will be reflected in vague research questions and a 'woolly' title. Here are some examples of rejected (a) and subsequently refined (b) titles:

1(a). A survey of appraisal in industry
(b). The management and improvement of appraisal systems in the Hightown Division of Berylmag Pharmaceuticals

2(a). Equine veterinary medicine
(b). A study of the changes in veterinary medicine resulting from increasing recreational horse riding

3(a). Temperature measurement in the steel industry
(b). A study of the accuracy and durability of refractory shielded thermocouples in blast furnaces

4(a). The popularity of small schools
(b). Marketing a small school: educational and social advantages as perceived by parents and stakeholders

You might like to consider whether the above need further polishing perhaps by the addition of a sub-title.

ASSESSING RELIABILITY, VALIDITY, GENERALISABILITY

These three concepts help provide blunt answers to the questions 'Is it any good; is it any use?' They are not the exclusive province of the positivist, scientific, quantitative researcher. The qualitative worker has to compete with what has been called 'The lure of numbers'—that is, the unjustified belief that data involving measurement are inherently more valuable than things that are observed or described. This prejudice makes it even more important for the qualitative researcher to subject all data to rigorous examination:

- **Reliability**: would the same procedures, experiments or actions carried out again produce the same result?
- **Validity**: are we actually measuring or observing what we claim to be?
- **Generalisability**: is our work applicable or useful to other people or situations?

The physical scientist may be required to provide complex mathematical or statistical analyses of the above, but the work of the social or educational researcher is also problematic. Compare the task of finding out whether one gramme of silver nitrate always yields the same amount of precipitate when treated with sodium chloride solution with that of discovering what percentage of residents in a village believe in God. All residents? What do you mean by 'believe'? Which God? Do they tell the truth? If reliability is checked by repeating the research in a year's time, is the sample the same although it is a year older?

These problems are not insuperable but must be acknowledged and considered to maintain academic integrity.

Beware of variables

Whenever human beings are involved it is very easy to produce apparently convincing research that is quite invalid because the **variables** are incorrectly identified. Suppose it is observed that people with tattoos are less successful in examinations than those without. An unwise researcher might spend time investigating the nature and physical effects of tattoos, whereas the true variables are certainly a complex mixture of social, psychological and attitudinal factors. The research would have no validity.

Try listing some factors that might influence the reliability and validity of research into the effects of alcohol on driving performance. You should have no difficulty in finding twenty. A critical approach to research can often uncover some surprising variables. If you were researching the occurrence of domestic house fires would you collect data on the presence of inflammable furniture, open fires and air flows in houses? Research by the Cheshire Fire Brigade, in 1992, showed that a major variable was the degree of family stress.

In pure experimental research you must clearly distinguish between the independent variables (those manipulated by the researcher) and the dependent variables (those which change as a result of the manipulation).

Generalisability, or generality in physical science, is particularly important to the social scientist. How far might the results of this work offer guidance or suggestions of practice to others in similar situations? Even such an apparently restricted study as title 1b above may enable readers to extrapolate to their own situation.

You may feel that your study is too brief or at too low a level to need attention to these concepts, but some understanding will pay dividends in assisting clarity of thought and purpose.

USING TUTORS AND SUPPORT

Practice varies widely among and within institutions. You may find one or more of the following tutorial practices:

- unspecified time on demand
- a stated time allocation
- some compulsory group or individual tutorials
- shared tutorial responsibility
- an initial tutorial only.

Find out the rules and, unless you are supremely confident, use the time. Experience over many years shows that failures and non-submissions are heavily dominated by those who have declined to see tutors. In addition, a top secret piece of advice: if you fail and appeal, the fact that you have not accepted tutorials will count against you. Most tutors take a fierce professional pride in their students and make themselves easily available; others may be more elusive.

It is vital to prepare for each tutorial by listing the areas that need discussion and the precise points that should be cleared up. If advice is sought about a particular chapter or section make sure that the tutor has been provided with a draft copy in advance. Do not make tape recordings of the session unless the tutor agrees.

Try to strike a friendly but strictly professional relationship. Some tutors refuse to make technical corrections to work as a matter of policy. You may have a preference which you can make known. Always try to space tutorials and amounts of script submitted; it is unfair to expect staff to deal effectively with thousands of words at short or non-existent notice.

ADOPTING HOUSE STYLES

As well as checking requirements, right from the start adopt the layout and format recommended by the institution, even in draft form. More stress is caused by wasting time on technical alterations than by making academic revisions.

In the absence of guidance, use the general pattern discussed in Chapter 3 and the conventions as follows:

- paper: white A4
- double space all main text, single space indented quotations
- fonts: plain and standard
- margins: 1.5 inches to the left, 1 inch elsewhere.

CHECKLIST

Have you:

- estimated the workload?
- clarified your research questions?
- written out a project schedule?
- understood what is specifically required?
- critically assessed your own proposals?
- considered the likely value and use of the work?
- made contact with your tutor?
- thought about your family, friends and personal life?

CASE STUDIES

Paul is encouraged to be realistic

On checking the university department's regulations Paul discovers that he is only allowed one tutorial for his project so he starts to organise a written submission. He quickly realises that his great idea is hopelessly over-ambitious and would probably tax a PhD student. This is confirmed by the tutor and together they settle on one research question focused on one site only: What are the immediate effects of small-scale open-cast mining on a small community from the social and environmental aspects?

On a weekend visit home he decides to visit the site but is told politely but firmly, 'No admittance without an official university letter of introduction'.

Alison focuses on marketing

Alison has decided that the central management problem facing her school over the next five years is that of marketing a denominational school in a highly competitive situation. Her family agrees that Saturday mornings, at least, will be a sacred writing day. The title suggested on her submission is 'Improving the marketing of a denominational high school: management problems and strategies'. The headteacher receives the idea enthusiastically—perhaps too enthusiastically—and her tutor accepts the focus. Several research questions emerge, the answers to which should have practical value to the school:

1. What are the perceptions of parents and stakeholders about educational standards at St Lucy's High School?

2. What factors are influencing parents to choose or reject the school?

3. What special problems occur in marketing denominational education?

4. How could management strategies for marketing be improved?

3
Getting Started

SELECTING YOUR RESEARCH METHODOLOGY

The basic question tackled here is 'How am I going to find out the answers?' The issue must be addressed by every student irrespective of the degree of formality required by the institution. At higher levels a complete justification of the approach is required including a survey of possibilities, a rationale for choice and an extensive review of the chosen method and its relation to the variables; a minimum requirement is an explanation of the reasons for the approach and its likely advantages and disadvantages.

The literature can be confusing in its terminology, especially in the use of the terms 'methodology' and 'method', sometimes interchangeably. Distinctions may also be found between 'strategies' and 'procedures'. You need to cover two areas: the **overall style** of the research and the **actual techniques** to be used within the empirical work.

Research falls into two basic styles which are **objective** and **subjective** (or nomothetic and idiographic). Objective approaches are concerned with physical characteristics and the external world,

universally applicable rules and laws, tested through hypothesis, experiment and survey. Subjective approaches deal with the created social lives of groups and individuals through observation and explanation: both are systematically controlled and empirical and may be used by physical or social scientists.

A term that students may find puzzling is *phenomenology*, which is an extreme subjectivist, qualitative mode of inquiry. The phenomenologist abandons all prior assumptions about the social world and does not test any hypothesis as this would automatically imply a preconception about the actors and the situation. This perspective demands a style which recognises the distortion due to the researcher in every situation. There are many levels of perceived reality in human experience which can be studied using subjectivist methods and techniques. A phenomenologist would not employ techniques such as structured interviews.

It is simply not true that the amateur researcher has the same freedom of choice as the professional. There are constraints of time, cost, access and ability amongst others but these need not demean the work providing academic integrity is maintained by acknowledgement of the limitations. More than one methodology may be used with areas of overlap.

The institution may specify a research method, for example the experimental method in pure science projects, or a limited range of methods. It is quite common in nursing and midwifery degrees to limit the student to **experimental, action or evaluative** approaches.

The student is not expected to write at length about the styles that have not been selected but to concentrate on the one that has. A brief outline of some possibilities follows.

Action research: sometimes called 'participative'

In this style the researcher tackles a real problem, intervenes, makes changes and monitors the effects. The subjects participate and implement the interventions, leading to further changes in a spiral pattern.

An example might be a hospital ward sister and staff investigating the effects of organisational changes on patient welfare and recovery rates over a three-year period, making changes to systems at regular intervals and modifying after each intervention. The sheer practical difficulties of such a project are immediately apparent.

General criticisms of action research include the lack of detachment of the participants, weak identification of variables, the time scales involved and the chance that the work may degenerate into haphazard tinkering. However, meticulous action research can product satisfying, 'real life' problem-solving.

Surveys

Surveys attempt to gather information from an entire group, or more usually a sample, which can then be used to make inferences or generate policy or reveal unsuspected facts. Students often grab at this one, as superficially the process seems easy. In fact, as in all research involving people, it can be a minefield. Even the last National Census mysteriously lost several million citizens!

The information may be gathered in several ways: for example, interviews, which are face-to-face exchanges with participants, and questionnaires, or structured lists of written inquiries, but it is easily invalidated by poor sampling and ambiguities (see Chapter 4). Students are often disappointed by very low response rates to their surveys but should realise that respondents may have little motivation to reply or may simply be irritated by the whole process if it is difficult to understand or too complex. Subjects may lie or try to please an interviewer and causality can never be proved: '20% of school pupils dislike school because of school uniform'.

Difficulties are neatly illustrated by two genuine quotations from research reports published in 1995:

> 'Although more than 3,500 questionnaires were delivered to tenants, who were offered the chance of winning a prize for taking part in the survey, only 373 completed questionnaires were returned.'

> 'The agents throughout North Staffordshire refused a request by health experts to send questionnaires to customers asking them if they had followed the advice on safe sunbathing.'

Surveys can be purely **descriptive**: how many males over 21 were unemployed at the end of 1994? or **explanatory**: what were the claimed reasons for unemployment? They can be purely for the collection of factual information or for decision-making. In the latter case there are some fairly complex mathematics used for determining sample size, measurement error and analysis of data.

If you are convinced that your study requires such treatment, specialist reading and tutorial help will be needed.

Remember that all data collection has a cost in money or time and that quite large extra costs may only result in minor improvements in the quality of the data obtained. Bluntly, only do what you have to do.

There may also be ethical factors: should the subjects be told of your intentions? should they be offered anonymity? how do you treat potentially sensitive biographical information? A great temptation to be avoided is the collection of great amounts of data that have little, if any, use. Do you really need dates of birth or marital status?

If the survey method is chosen you must critically analyse the proposals:

- What hypothesis is being tested or developed?
- How does the literature illuminate this?
- How could the study be designed to provide the best data?
- What instruments are appropriate?
- How will the survey be checked and piloted?
- Is the sample representative?
- What is going to be done with the answers?

Poor quality surveys often represent the worst of research. A 1994 'professional' survey concluded that the people of a northern industrial city were aimless and apathetic, based on a sample of 10!

Experimental method

Experimental method is used in all types of research but in its 'pure' form is associated principally with work in the physical sciences. Some argue that all studies outside the range of physical science are more accurately described as quasi-experiments.

The process, in outline, is the formulation of an hypothesis based on observation and theory that can be tested and proved or refuted. Independent variables are precisely manipulated to prove causal effects on dependent variables. The whole is characterised by precision, accurate measurement and careful duplication which should enable exact prediction and generality. Such purity is rarely found in practice and many great scientific discoveries have been made by accident or serendipity.

Experiment in the social sciences faces difficult issues of control, ethics and external validity. Empirical knowledge about people—numbers, ages, heights etc—is often what interests us least, whereas beliefs and attitudes defy measurement.

Suppose an experiment is set up to test the hypothesis that children's reading development is proportional to numbers of books available in classrooms. Apart from the difficulties of ensuring equal starting points, equal motivation and equal ability there is the insuperable ethical problem of setting up a control group which is completely deprived of books!

Nevertheless, there have been many fascinating and useful experiments with people, especially in the field of psychology. Even in this discipline where tight control is exercised, samples mature or are 'lost', practice changes results and the well-known Hawthorne Effect occurs where the behaviour of subjects alters when they know that they are taking part in an experiment.

Ethnographic research

This is a qualitative, descriptive style in which a researcher attempts a study of the behaviour and customs of a group of people by integration into the society. The method has produced many riveting studies but is unlikely to be recommended to many students as it is time consuming and the procedures are actually very complex.

Criticisms often made of the value of ethnographic work include: it is unscientific, it is not generalisable, the personality of the researcher causes bias, small groups are unrepresentative. Proponents would say that all these are outweighed by the value of dense observations of real life.

Ethical questions abound. In a well-known study of gang culture the integration of the researcher collapsed when he was asked to commit a serious crime. You may have already rejected ethnographic method but do at least consider the general principles as they illuminate all qualitative work. The constant rivalry between 'hard' quantitative approaches and 'soft' qualitative ones has led to the latter developing a complex epistemology (theory of the basis of knowledge) and some highly structured ways of recording data. Ethnomethodology attempts to analyse communication, its sequence and meaning. Even pauses and hesitations are transcribed in a notation system and linked with the setting. Fascinating, but only to be tried under expert tutorial guidance.

Case study

Perhaps the commonest approach but also the most abused, this is a study concerning one particular happening, or case, examining events and facets of the focused area in a meticulous and systematic way. This latter point must be stressed as poor case studies often degenerate into unstructured descriptions of randomly chosen features.

Case study is often classified as 'qualitative by definition' but quantitative techniques can be used. The hypotheses usually emerge from the study, although a careful conceptual framework should be present at the start. Avoid scattering data like confetti.

A vivid realisation of structures, power, hierarchies and unsuspected variables may result which can be generalisable to similar situations depending on the uniqueness of the focus. However, resist the temptation to make universal theories out of trivia. It is probable that the researcher will have some involvement with the case and this should set alarm bells ringing about the danger of subjectivity.

A social worker may refer to one person or one family as a case study but for a dissertation the term refers to a recognisable area such as a factory, school or department with definable boundaries. There is inevitably overlap with other styles and case study may be termed a procedure or technique rather than a style.

Historical research

For most students this will mean the use of historical or documentary sources to illuminate a contemporary problem. It requires the same academic rigour as all other methods and may be more difficult to carry out. If you intend to use this method its acceptability must be checked with the tutor. Some questions to be considered include:

- What is the exact problem to be investigated?
- Is there a hypothesis to be tested?
- Is it intended to discover new knowledge?
- What sources will be used?
- Can they be accessed?

For example, a student proposed a draft title 'The effects of changing policies on local authority planning permissions since 1974'. Apart from the vagueness about the locus and scope of the work, it is possible but would require access to Planning Committee minutes, Government papers, perhaps even local newspaper archives. Such a workload is certainly beyond the scope of a single researcher.

Documentary analyses may be combined with other styles of research or to provide background data in case studies. Like surveys this seems to have a great attraction for students who often, unfortunately, take it to mean the description of the contents of a document. There must be a closely defined system, a series of questions to answer and a set of categories to analyse. For example, a researcher posing the question, 'How is time allocated in a Council committee?' from recorded minutes, might use the categories:

- reports from other sources
- members' questions
- non-agenda matter
- matters for action.

A tally sheet instrument is necessary to record the occurrences.

Correlational research

This is research where the variables are studied for possible relationships without manipulating them, unlike the experimental style. Obviously causation cannot be proved but it can be implied. Mathematical correlations are used to show the degree of association between the two or more variables chosen and high correlations may allow predictions or point the way to experiments.

Areas that have been researched in this style include the relationship between divorce rates and social class, and smoking, lung cancer and life style.

There are always threats to the validity of such studies by the intrusion of unrecognised variables.

Evaluative research

This style of research, which is often commissioned professionally, deals principally with questions of social policy and activity answering such questions as:

- Are stated plans and policies being carried out?
- Is what is being done worth doing?

- Are success criteria being attained?
- Can achievements be clarified and categorised?
- Is there a gap between intention and implementation?

Although evaluative work needs to be highly structured, if judgements of worthwhileness are made the skill and status of the researcher become vital issues. In fact this latter point applies to all amateur work and will be considered briefly in this chapter.

Making your choice and sticking to it

As interesting as the many research styles are, having chosen and justified an approach on rational grounds, you must concentrate on that methodology both in reading and writing while maintaining an awareness of the different paradigms.

THE RESEARCHER'S STATUS

Much university and college research is of excellent quality but it is still amateur, except for some PhD and postdoctoral students who may be paid. Status can be enhanced by following some simple, obvious rules which students often ignore:

1. Give yourself a legitimate title, eg Mrs Alison French, MA Research Student of Anytown University.

2. Adopt a polite, professional manner in dealing with all contacts.

3. Dress well when doing your field work: people still have prejudices about students.

4. Word process all communications to a high standard.

5. Keep a generally formal tone; people can be suspicious of chattiness.

6. Explain to those involved what are your general intention and purpose.

7. Offer to share results where appropriate.

Your status will also be affected by the quality of your research instruments. This will be returned to in a later section.

SAMPLING

This is potentially a very complex business with many traps for the unwary. It is basically the obtaining of a manageable part of an object or population that supposedly possesses the same qualities as the whole. The physical world presents fewer problems than the social one; it is easier to obtain a one gramme sample from a tonne of limestone than to get an accurate sample of a hundred unemployed people.

The student has a duty to ensure that:

- the sample is large enough to be significant
- it is as representative as possible
- its defects are acknowledged
- a rationale for it is produced.

The smaller the sample the less is the generalisability of the results. A lot of defective research results from attempting to extrapolate from tiny samples to grand theory. We may be forced by circumstances to use the only sample that can be reached—an **opportunity** sample. Commonly used are **random** samples but the randomness is often more apparent than real. For example, there are different numbers of people whose surnames begin with each letter. Taking the third name from every school register may result in an all male sample. Choosing respondents at one time of day may mean that you have all commuters or all school children. Large random samples may be best produced by using computer generated lists of random numbers.

There is no definite answer to the question 'How large should a sample be?' This requires judgement of feasibility and cost against representativeness. There is no point in taking huge samples when smaller ones produce the same results.

Other types of sample include **stratified** where a layer is selected, for example 50-year-olds only who are supposed to possess the same characteristics as those in the general 50-year-old population; **matched** samples where two groups are found as alike as possible or **clusters** which are groups defined by area or environment. Further sophistications may be built in such as random sampling within a cluster. **Systematic sampling** is the selection of names at a given interval, say, every tenth house in a street. Such a sample has the potential to be very biased, for example there may be 25 old people's bungalows.

Even a 'given' sample as in a small case study should be described and justified.

Try answering the following questions about a real research project:

> The UK Co-ordinating Committee on Cancer Research is investigating the value of screening women for breast cancer. Their sample is 200,000 symptom-free women in their forties, comparing those who are given mammograms with those who are not, at many different centres, over 13 years or more.
>
> 1. Is the sample large enough?
> 2. What kind of sample is it?
> 3. Can you foresee any problems with the sample?

FOLLOWING GENERAL PATTERNS

Your organisation may give precise guidance about the structure of the dissertation but is more likely to allow some freedom. You will find it a powerful help and incentive to have a framework of chapters or sections with indications of the proposed contents. This can be refined and modified as the work proceeds.

A typical dissertation will have between five and eight chapters on the general lines below.

STRUCTURING YOUR DISSERTATION

Introduction

What is going to be done? Why are you doing it? Who is likely to be interested in it? What exactly is the hypothesis or problem? What is the possible use of the research? What is the locus and focus?

Literature review

What have others said, written or researched about your topic? What theories illuminate your topic? How does the literature relate to your research questions?

Research methodology

How will you approach the empirical work? What style and techniques have been chosen? Why? What samples, tests, observations and measurements will be needed?

Data analysis

What data have been found? What is your interpretation of them? Do they prove or refute an hypothesis?

Conclusions

How can you summarise the work? Are there any actions or recommendations to take? Was it all successful?

Bibliography

What books, journals, papers and other sources have been referred to throughout the work?

Appendices

Are there any extra details that the specialist reader could refer to if necessary?

The above may be modified according to the subject area and the style of research but the general pattern holds good. Some institutions prefer to split the dissertation into three sections:

- rationale and design
- methodology and data collection
- analysis and conclusions.

Generally speaking, the smaller the number of recommended sections the harder students find it to organise their work. This is especially true where the literature review is supposedly dispersed through two sections or is described by the institution as a 'theoretical analysis'.

Whatever the area—science, arts, education or social science—you will be required to demonstrate:

- extensive and relevant reading
- an understanding of the theories that underpin the research
- meticulous empirical work
- a knowledge of academic conventions
- the ability to report effectively.

READING FOR A DEGREE

'Reading' for a degree is the traditional expression which meant taking a degree and it reflects the dominance of reading in the process. The whole dissertation should show the evidence of wide and up-to-date use of literature from the introduction to the conclusion. Some lucky people can read anywhere and in any conditions; most can not. Finding reading time is difficult in a busy college and is even more difficult if you have a house to clean and small children to look after. Some simple tactics may help.

Planning your time

Short, fragmented sessions tend to be of little use. Two hours is more productive and an occasional complete library day will be essential. It is necessary to plan reading just like the empirical work with careful note-making and recording. A ruthless approach will help you avoid drowning in a sea of books. Never read aimlessly, hoping that something will show up. Use the contents and indices of your possible sources and read only directly relevant material which may be one chapter or less.

Your references may be drawn from books, journals, periodicals, newspapers or any appropriate source but remember that all subject-specific books date rapidly. Some standard works remain almost permanently relevant, but be wary of anything more than five years old. Journals offer a better chance of reports on more recent studies.

Before travelling any long distance to a library, telephone to check the availability of what you are hoping to use. Books in heavy demand may be 'frozen', that is on temporary reference or on a shorter loan period than normal. Some libraries have reciprocal arrangements with others and permit borrowing by another college's students: if not, most can organise inter-library loans and materials from the British Library. Periodicals may only be available in the library and not for loan.

Recording your reading

It is essential that for every work consulted you record in your note book:

- the name of the author or authors
- the full title
- the edition, if not the first
- the publisher
- the date of publication
- the ISBN number
- the library classification
- page number, if very specific.

For journals and periodicals it is also necessary to record the volume and number and always the page numbers.

As these are recorded it is very useful to log with the details the reason why the book was consulted and a note of sections that may be returned to later, parts that you intend to use or quote from and actual quotations that may feature in the literature review. If possible, handle each book once only. The reason for this is obvious when you remember that an average master's thesis contains 90 references.

Start with the general theoretical and background books and progress to very precise and recent work which is likely to be concentrated in journals.

I have seen some very effective systems for colour coding details of books using coloured inserts or dividers in loose-leaf folders; for example, red for literature review, green for research methods, blue for quotations. If you are fast and confident with a PC, equivalent systems can be developed using different fonts, bold, or italics. Do not be over complex: go for simplicity in all your systems.

With luck, your first few books should set off a chain reaction as their bibliographies lead you to related work. Be selective and not over ambitious at first as the literature may divert you to a different emphasis. When you feel ready for a literature search there are several exciting possibilities.

Almost every subject area has indexes to periodicals, official publications and reports such as the Business Periodicals Index and the General Science Index. Most are available on CD-ROM and often cover the USA and Europe. These need to have a planned access as the main problem is information overload. Feed in the word 'Education' and you may get 10,000 references! Add the additional key words 'infant' and 'deafness' and a manageable total emerges. As with most aspects of a dissertation the vital concept is focus.

If you have access to the Internet you may find references and contacts, especially in American universities, but be warned, the potential for information overload is even greater than on CD-ROM. A genuine example of a search gave the following numbers of references:

Nursing	430,024
+ Children	30,000
+ Mental	10,000
+ Autism	400
+ Staffordshire	1

Some more practical advice on this theme is found in Chapter 5.

CHECKLIST

Have you:

- considered your overall research style?
- chosen and justified a definite methodology?
- formulated an hypothesis where appropriate?
- categorised your sample?
- thought of the total pattern of the dissertation and its relationship to the research questions?
- planned your reading programme?
- cleared all the above, where possible, with the tutor?

CASE STUDIES

Paul opts for a case study

With some difficulty, Paul has obtained a letter of introduction as asked for by the open-cast site manager. He has decided that the work will be a qualitative case study with strong possibilities of being generalisable to other, similar situations. The tutor seems unhappy that some of the quantitative techniques taught on the course will not be used but agrees to the outline and points Paul to the excellent selection of literature held in the department and to articles in the journal *Mining Engineer*. He makes a start on the reading and plans a field visit.

Alison decides on a survey

Alison has decided that survey will be her principal approach and that she will use a mixture of qualitative and quantitative styles. There may be a problem with the sample sizes for her first two research questions and in view of the nature of the institution the validity of the study may be in doubt. She can see the overall pattern of the dissertation but is rather taken aback that, by the time it takes her to read the general marketing theory, a month has slipped by.

4
Techniques

THE TOOL BOX

All research requires techniques and instruments for the collection of data. Even historical research needs a structured framework for the collection of details. The wide range of possibilities includes logs, diaries, tests, tally sheets, questionnaires and interviews which further sub-divide into categories. In addition some choice exists within the mechanical methods of writing, film, video, tape-recording and computer disk.

As ever the real choice has constraints defined by the type of research, time, cost and the nature of the data being sought. There must be careful matching of the instruments to the questions being researched.

You may collect the data entirely yourself, from the people being studied or from a secondary source, and the actual instruments may be devised by yourself or professionally produced. Remember that the latter are copyright and their use can involve a cost. Despite this, if it is proposed to administer standard type tests such as personality inventories in psychology, you are strongly advised to consider professional ones as they will have been piloted, developed and modified over a long period to a level of refinement which is beyond the capacity of students to match in self-developed instruments.

It is perfectly practicable to develop your own research instruments as long as you realise that it is more difficult than it seems and needs a meticulous, critical process.

Every time that field work of any description is undertaken it is wise to take notes of dates, names, places, the type of work, in addition to your results and observations. You will forget!

Some instruments are highly specific to a particular task and you should seek specialist advice on these. It may also be permissible

TYPES OF PUPIL BEHAVIOUR	
Observed behaviour	**Frequency**
Writing	
Reading	
No activity	
Talking to another pupil	
Talking to the teacher	
Disruptive behaviour	
Personal activity	

Fig. 3. A sample tally sheet.

to submit them in an electronic form: for example, video recordings in sports science research or student-devised software programs.

Do not administer research instruments that require highly skilled interpretation such as picture completions or sociograms unless you are confident of your ability.

MAKING OBSERVATIONS

Observational techniques, used principally for qualitative research, require a highly structured set-up—perhaps more so as they are open to charges of subjectivity. The group being studied is identified as a **purposive sample** by the researcher as is the episode or behaviour to be observed.

The researcher may adopt different levels of participation from being a complete participant to being completely detached. The former can cause difficulties in using written lists or check boxes. It is often argued that the very presence of an observer means that the episode being studied is different from a 'normal' situation. However, this applies, in different degrees, to all research except physical experiments.

Self-devised tally sheets and checklists should be clear, concise and unobtrusive. Figure 3 shows an example from a student studying classroom behaviour.

Presumably, the student intends to define the categories shown. What is 'disruptive behaviour' or 'personal activity'? What periods of time are involved? How is it possible to observe an entire class? The sample illustrates how easy it is to invalidate an instrument and warns that what might be blindingly obvious to the researcher is not so to the reader.

Making observations should always involve a two-stage process:

- recording the 'raw' data in the note book or log sheet at the episode site

- reflecting on and considering the collected data at a later time.

PREPARING QUESTIONNAIRES

Supervisors tend to turn pale when students say things like 'I'll just knock up a questionnaire'. So tempting as they can be relatively easy to administer and reasonably cheap, but they are full of traps for the unwary. The fundamental rule is that every respondent needs to understand what is required in the precise sense that the researcher meant it. Normally a pilot run is used to show or confirm this fact—it rarely does. If for any reason a pilot is not possible, then the minimum acceptable is 'piloting' with a tutor.

Try to see the questionnaire from the recipient's point of view. Are they likely to be interested in it or co-operative? How could they be encouraged? Some commercial marketing organisations include a free draw with their questionnaire and still get low responses. Remember that a low return rate may have research significance and has to be reported. You will be fortunate if you reach a 70% rate of response on personally collected questionnaires and postal ones may be as low as 10%. Various follow-up methods can improve matters but cause delays and increased cost and could conceivably invalidate the results by making an intended cross-sectional study into a longitudinal one, that is a study of the same population repeated over a period of time.

Structuring your questions

Language used by the researcher must be **simple, direct** and **appropriate** to the target population.

Attempt to relate each question to your research questions or hypothesis and you will find that many can be edited out. Also remember that if the scoring system for the answers is complex, extra hours may be required that are not budgeted for.

People hate confusing questions that demand different styles of response from one part to the next: ticks followed by circles followed by writing. Also irritating are changes in the format of questions. It is better to have a 'house style' for the whole questionnaire.

Closed-end questionnaires are easier to administer and to score but can produce bland or sterile answers for example:

> Which of the following Leisure Centre facilities have you actually used? (tick)
>
> ☐ swimming pool
>
> ☐ multigym

- ☐ sports hall
- ☐ outdoor field
- ☐ none of these

Simple multiple choice questions almost always need a 'none of these' or 'don't know' or 'other' category.

Other scales may be used but some target populations find these difficult to cope with; for example, Likert scales:

> 'The Leisure Centre provides good facilities for mothers with small children'
> Tick the statement that best describes your opinion:
> 1 strongly disagree 2 disagree 3 neither agree nor disagree 4 agree 5 strongly agree

This type of question does not cover respondents who are not sure or who have no opinion.

Scales that require complex instructions only work well with targets who are involved and committed to the research, for example **semantic differential**:

> Place a vertical mark on the line between the two words that may describe your attitude towards some features of the Leisure Centre. For example, if you feel that the atmosphere is friendly put your mark near to that word.
> friendly . . . / . . . / . . . / . . . / . . . / . . . / . . . / . . . / unfriendly

In this case it seems that the information obtained does not merit the complexity of the instrument and again there is no scope for the respondent who thinks that the atmosphere is downright hostile!

Open-ended questions offer the respondent a variety of responses:

> 'What is your opinion of the facilities for mothers with small children?'

Such a question may produce deep, insightful answers but equally may result in a difficult to read 'All right' or 'OK'. Single researchers could easily introduce a bias at the analysis stage.

The unsatisfactory wording of the semantic differential question above illustrates how slippery words in questions can be. Vagueness breeds vagueness:

> 'Are you acquainted with the facilities?'
> 'Do you generally use the swimming pool?'

What does 'acquainted' mean? Have heard about them? Used them? 'Generally' is a very common word in students' questionnaires which means very little. It is very easy to build in disastrous ambiguities:

> 'Do you enjoy travelling via the Channel Tunnel and the ferries?'
> Answer: Well, yes and no sometimes.

Questions should not lead the respondent by assuming a particular stance:

> 'Are the severe government cuts responsible for . . . ?'

Questionnaires, more than any other instrument, need the application of the 'so what?' test. You need constantly to relate every section to your research questions. Questionnaires that I have seen recently seem to be full of questions like:

> 'Do you think that tutors should take an interest in students?'
> 'Do you agree that seminar rooms should be warm and comfortable?'

These two were followed by a Likert scale ranging from 'strongly agree' to 'strongly disagree'. If the research question was, 'What factors influence drop-out rates from university courses?' the data collected will have little relevance to providing an answer that was not blindingly obvious already.

Despite all these strictures a good questionnaire can be invaluable for producing large amounts of valid, handleable data with a high degree of objectivity.

Introducing your questionnaire

Never distribute unheaded, unexplained questionnaires. As a

minimum the heading should state the origin and purpose of the work; more extensive questionnaires should have a letter attached in which the overall purpose of the research is outlined, brief details of availability of results are given and official contacts are named.

CONDUCTING INTERVIEWS

Interviewing is a method of collecting data that can stand on its own or be a follow-up process to another method. Interviews should never be random as they demand a heavy investment of time. One comparatively short interview can take an hour to organise, an hour to carry out and half an hour to reflect on.

Interviews can also save a lot of time if used as preparation for the structure of other research. The researcher's perception of reality may not correspond with that of the target subjects: a pilot interview can reveal this quickly. Here are examples of such questions:

> 'As a departmental manager what are your three greatest problems in personnel management?'
> 'Which processes do you think need review and change?'

An interview is not a conversation but a structured way of obtaining information on a focused content. The basic choice is between structured or unstructured interviews but even so-called unstructured interviews have structure, however minimal.

The **structured** interview uses standard pre-designated questions which enable the responses of different individuals to be compared. Sometimes the outline schedule is communicated to the interviewee prior to the interview. An excessively rigid structure may raise the point, why not just use a questionnaire? A semi-structured approach may elicit startling and personal information that changes the entire development of the work.

Inevitably, the less the structure, the greater the skill is required for interpretation and the greater the potential for interviewer bias. Consider the different implications of the tones of the following:

> 'Is the budget balanced for 1998?'
> 'Is the **budget** balanced for 1998?'
> 'Surely you have balanced the budget for 1998?'

You will be expected to give very precise details of the interview process in the dissertation and to acknowledge any weaknesses. Apart from the structural constitution of the interview, many aspects need to be considered including:

- the **personality** of the interviewer
- the **time** control
- the **location** and total environment of the interview
- shared **knowledge** of interviewer and interviewee
- **techniques** of data collection and analysis.

These may be seen to add weight to the phenomenological case for each interview being a unique episode.

The notes about the researcher's status apply strongly to interviewers as you will only draw out information compatible with your status. Occasionally this presents an insuperable barrier, for example, an 18-year-old student interviewing a chief executive, or a male interviewing a Moslem woman. It should also be noted that interviewing children may require parental permission.

Recording the data

It is important to give some thought to the actual recording of the data. All technology seems to influence the process, in my experience even telephone interviewing has a strange effect. Some interviewees are paralysed with fright at a tape recorder or video camera. Be aware of these effects and always ask permission to use them. A note book and pen still offers a viable option and this should be used discreetly, perhaps on the knee. Some students develop a highly effective shorthand system where every question and response is coded or numbered.

The actual physical circumstances of the interview are important. Critics of the validity of the process argue that each interview is a unique social episode and they have a point if one interview is carried out in a noisy corridor and one in a quiet study. The researcher may set certain ground rules and if these are broken the data are rejected.

Interviews can be destroyed by ringing telephones, uncomfortable chairs and noise. Record all the environmental factors and be prepared to report on them.

Considerable interpersonal and interpretational skills are necessary to detect nervousness or hostility, to interpret body language, to link the questions and to probe sensitively. You should not be thrown by all these problems but need an honest awareness of them.

The potential density of interview material is illustrated by this real, recorded answer to a question about pupil assaults on teachers:

> '. . . I've been hit once, when I was separating a fight. I was separating a fight and somebody was swinging a punch at the adversary and I got it on the chin—but that was an accident, there was definitely no way he could have meant it.'

A questionnaire item might have read:

> 'Have you ever been struck by a pupil? Yes/No'

What do you make of the repetition of the phrase '. . . separating a fight'? What about the tone of '. . . got it on the chin'? Does it appear unusual for a person to use the words 'adversary' and 'no way' together?

Consider some of the types of questions that can be used and their likely results:

1. Have you worked at the hospital for more than five years?

2. How satisfied are you with working conditions?

3. Can we now consider union activity?

4. You blamed poor management for the problems: could you elaborate on that?

5. Would you like to say anything else about working here?

Which of these questions might be classified as open-ended, closed, probing, leading or interviewer controlled?

A summary of the rules for interviewer conduct

- Be friendly but formal.
- Follow your schedule.

- Treat all interviewees the same.
- Prompt without directing.
- Do not volunteer answers.
- Avoid all innuendo or irony.
- Never be patronising or pompous.
- Develop your status.
- Be tolerant and patient.

Interview Schedule for Parents

Q7 (*exact wording for all*) Here are some comments that parents have made about St Lucy's. Would you tell me if you share these opinions or not?
(*read in as neutral a way as possible*)

	A	D	NO
(a) The discipline is generally good			
(b) Rigid uniform adds to the tone of the school			
(c) Exam results are satisfactory			
(d) Communication with parents is unsatisfactory			
(e) The reputation of the school is excellent			

Q8 Can we now talk about the reasons why you sent your own children to St Lucy's? (*prompt if no response, academic work, social reasons, Catholic ethos*)

Q9 Would you like to say a little more about your main reason? (*allow to talk freely*)

A = agree D = disagree NO = no opinion

Look at the extract from Alison's semi-structured interview schedule (see page opposite). Check whether these relate to Alison's research questions (see Chapter 2).

NEGOTIATING WITH PEOPLE

Whatever the selected style of research it will inevitably require negotiating with others. Even the physical scientist needs access to laboratories, sites and technology. Remember that the research, so dear to you, may be an irritant to others and is, at best, an intrusion on their time. Fortunately, most people are kind and helpful if approached correctly. The following general tips are derived from experience:

- All communications to be of a high standard and quality.
- If possible, check names and statuses beforehand.
- Be friendly but formal.
- Explain what you intend to do.
- Offer to make results available if possible.
- Work to your target's time limitations, not yours.
- Cultivate your legitimate status (see Chapter 3).

Figures 4(a) and (b) show two examples of student communications. Have the two students followed the 'rules'? Can you improve them in any way?

[Questionnaire heading]

Dear Colleague

You may know that I am researching for a Master's thesis, at Midshire University, on marketing at St Lucy's school. It is hoped that the results will be of practical use to us.

It would be a great help if you could spare a few minutes to complete the attached questionnaire and return it to my pigeon hole. Please ask if you need any further details.

Thank you for your help at this busy time.

Yours sincerely

Alison B . . .

Fig. 4. (a) A sample covering letter.

Rm, 23
Croft Bld
University of . . .
Northshire
6th March 199X

Mr B. Martin, Site Controller
Geomine Plc
Highfield OCM
Stanton

Dear Mr Martin

You may recall our telephone conversation last month about my research into the effects of open-cast mining on a small community, as part of my BSc degree studies. The project has been approved by Professor J. Cookson and I hope that it will be possible for me to make a visit to the site as you suggested, when it is convenient for you. Perhaps you could indicate a suitable date and time.

I would be pleased to offer you a copy of the report when completed.

Yours sincerely

Paul W . . .

Fig. 4. (b) A sample covering letter.

CHECKLIST

Have you:

- set up a system for field work recording?
- decided how the data are to be collected?
- chosen the exact instruments and related them to your research questions?
- critically checked for problems and ambiguities?
- piloted where appropriate?
- negotiated with your targets?

CASE STUDIES

Paul expands his workload

Paul carried out the site visit and the manager was extremely helpful, providing a tour of the area and giving Geomine's perspective on their activities, maps and literature and useful quantitative data. He was allowed to take photographs. Paul has decided to use the information from the site manager and to interview all five farmers and smallholders whose land was affected by the scheme and to select a systematic 20 per cent sample of the 57 houses that back directly onto the open-cast area. He decided to attempt structured interviews with these householders. The houses seem to be of similar type. Meanwhile he intends to write up the introduction and literature review.

Alison runs into difficulties

Alison has now written 4,000 words and has left the literature review to write up research methodology, partly to clarify her own thinking on this. It works because it helps her to define the sample and three target groups for the survey: staff, parents and governors. Unfortunately, her tutor is not happy with the introduction, which has to be rewritten, and her family is not keeping to the agreement about study time!

5
Down to Details

By this stage all the careful planning should be paying off but also some little waves of panic may be felt. Minor issues seem to take hours and the empirical work refuses to behave neatly. Keep your nerve. If you are held up by unforseen circumstances do not elect for a blank spell but work on another task such as the bibliography or the polishing of the literature review. It helps to have your own job list and to tick off each section as completed. Try to put as much as possible in its final or near final form. If the sheer volume of work daunts you consider chopping out some of the areas of lower priority and restricting the scope of the empirical work to a sharper focus. Remember that however great your problems, it is certain that others have experienced the same or worse and have still completed the dissertation and passed!

THE INTRODUCTION: SETTING OUT YOUR STALL

Some writers write the **introduction** first, some at the end. It is better to do both! That is write it first and edit it at the end. Writing the introduction is a valuable way of:

- clarifying thoughts
- breaking the ice
- establishing a style
- providing a basis for a tutorial.

It also provides between seven and ten per cent of your dissertation in a fairly painless way.

The introduction should show, in outline, what has prompted the research: such things as government legislation, industrial change, need for improvement, search for new knowledge, policy change, evaluation. It should then go on to state concisely what it is intended to do, what the research questions or hypotheses are and where the research is to be located.

The style should be scholarly, clear and direct with several references to key, general texts that deal with your basic theories. Quite a good way to start is with a vivid, pithy quotation from one of these texts. For example:

> 'I'm not going to have the monkeys running the zoo.'
> (Former Chairman, Eastern Airlines, discussing worker participation, 1986)
>
> Modern human resource management systems have recognised that the monkeys may actually be quite effective at running the zoo but may need more than bananas for motivation.
>
> (This introduction then goes on to describe briefly some other research into worker participation in decision-making, outlines the necessity for evaluative work and the importance of proper management of human resources. It then delineates the exact intention of the researcher, the research questions and the proposed style of the study.)

You may consider that the above opening is too joky or glib, if so then edit it out and change it. Severely limit all humorous or facetious remarks and if in doubt, remove them.

A few relevant quotations from general sources will help to establish the right tone at the beginning.

WRITING YOUR LITERATURE REVIEW

The **literature review** is central to the dissertation and in all styles of work it has a number of functions:

- It shows that you have read widely around your chosen topic.
- It demonstrates your critical understanding of the theory.
- It acknowledges the work of others.
- It informs and modifies your own research.

Your main problem will be to balance correctly the use of quotation from the work of others with critical gloss and evaluative comment of your own. A common fault in literature reviews is to sprinkle references liberally around with insufficient thought as to how they fit in to the theory and the theme. Every time a work is referred to or a quotation included apply the mental test 'So what?' In other words, what is this reference adding to the development of my theory; how does it follow the thread of the dissertation and how does it relate to my research questions?

When transferring your notes on the literature into the actual literature review, check the reasons why each reference will illuminate or complement your work. One or more of the following must apply:

- It deals with theory that underpins your work.
- It makes a definitive statement about an aspect of your study.
- It deals with your subject area or overlaps it.
- It shows your acknowledgement of the work of others.
- It assists in the maintenance of a coherent argument.
- It puts your work into an external context.
- It defines the current state of research in your area.

It is rare that a quotation will stand entirely on its own without relating it to your own work. While students should have a healthy respect for the great seminal works in their field (I once saw an A Level answer that began '*Hamlet* is crap'!) this does not mean that the student should not critically discuss the application of them to the current research or even claim that they have been superseded by others. It can be particularly effective to examine the propositions of rival theorists, especially if one corresponds with your own stance.

A very common problem found in literature reviews is the tendency to let them drift away from the rest of the dissertation and become separate scholarly essays which, while they may have an intrinsic interest, do not underpin the empirical work. Avoid this by trying the 'So what?' test at the bottom of every page.

The 'pencil sharpening' image used in Chapter 1 holds good for the pattern of the literature review. General background and standard theoretical works should be concentrated into the early pages. As the review develops, references should become more specific to the exact topic, use more journals and periodicals which are up-to-date and current, move from theory to practice and finish with a direct lead-in to your own empirical work.

In the actual writing the style should be clear and direct. Subheadings may help this and also discourage deviation.

Introducing your references

There are several ways to introduce the chosen references; all should be included to ensure smoothness, variety and readability:

1. *Acknowledged paraphrase of an author's words or ideas*

   Edirisinghe (1989) explored the injection moulding of ceramics using several thermoplastic binders. He found . . .

2. *Brief, exact quotations incorporated within the student's text*

   The difficulty of investigating the processes in elite groups, attributed by Delamonte (1993) to the 'inverted snobbery of sociologists' is described as the . . .

3. *Full quotations of more than one line, separated from the main text and usually single spaced which makes inverted commas unnecessary:*

> The political stance of many ecologists has shifted from the
>
> left to a new green centre. This has meant some personal
>
> agonising.
>
> When the forms of an old culture are dying, the new culture is created by a few people who are not afraid to be insecure.
>
> (Bahro 1984)

Some abbreviations are useful but should be used sparingly in your text:

1. *Ibid* (in the same place). It is used to avoid repeating an author's name where the reference is from the same work as the immediately previous one.
2. *Op Cit* (the work already referred to). Not much use as it is a source of possible ambiguity unless the author's name is given.

3. *Loc Cit* (the place cited). More specific: not only the same work but the same place in it.
4. *Sic* (thus). Used if you want to quote something with a mistake in it that you do not want to be attributed to yourself.
5. *Et al* (and others). Takes the place of all but the first in a list of multiple authors.

It is very important to maintain the thread of purpose throughout the literature review (as it is during the entire dissertation) and also to make sure that the reader senses this. Here is an example of a quotation, followed by a critical gloss and an implied reference to a research question:

> *The sociocultural domain describes the general values and mores of a society but the people of a society are the actual customers of an organisation . . . Managers should focus managerial strategies primarily on current and potential customers rather than on the general beliefs, values and mores of society as a whole.*
>
> (Dunham and Pierce 1989)

> Such a description no doubt fits a commercial, profit-orientated organisation but the position in an educational organisation may be quite different. The customers are often more concerned to 'purchase' a perceived value system, either that of society or the school itself, rather than a tangible object. The school can be marketing its own sociocultural system either in conjunction with or possibly opposed to that of society.

In using the research data of others do not repeat their data but comment on their basic findings as they illuminate what you propose to do.

While footnotes may be necessary in some scientific papers, in general they should not be used and certainly not for bibliographic references. A system for this latter purpose is explained later.

Consider here, too, giving each chapter or section a title other than the bald 'Literature Review'. For example, The Economics of Choice: Research and Impact Over Five Years.

Remember, it is extremely rare for anyone who writes a good literature review to fail on their dissertation!

WRITING ABOUT RESEARCH METHODS

Check the institution's requirements in dealing with **research methods**. Some ask for a separate chapter; some suggest incorporation into the introduction. There may be other variants but no piece of research at any level will be convincing unless the writer explains:

- why a particular method has been chosen
- what are the characteristics of the population, sample or experiment
- why some possibilities have been rejected
- what instruments will be used.

There are several dangers involved in this deceptively easy process. The first one has already been mentioned in connection with the literature review, that is making the chapter sound detached from the rest of the work. Again, make several references to the research question or problem.

Do not waste valuable time in complex descriptions of methods that have not been chosen for reasons which are patently obvious. For example, it is pointless for Paul to discuss the use of action research as his time scale does not allow it and it is clearly an inappropriate method. Likewise, a physical scientist does not need to agonise over ethnography. There may be two or three styles available to you and you should be honest about the constraints. Concentrate on the selected style and explore its potential advantages and disadvantages as they relate to your study. Include in the section references to the research literature. For example:

> The interviews will be semi structured and a number of difficulties will have to be overcome:
>
> There seems to be a temptation to think of interviews rather like thermometers—they can be conveniently inserted almost anywhere within the body of the research and simply read off to provide a series of trustworthy observations.
>
> (Powney & Watts 1987)

To increase the validity of the interviews in this research . . .

PRESENTING AND ANALYSING DATA

Consider first the amount of **data** that has been collected and secondly the level of measurement involved. Large quantities of data will need summary in one form or another. Some types of data require high-level statistics and the student should find suitable specialist help or literature for this. However, many dissertations are ruined by spurious statistics based on poor or inadequate sampling. Is there any real point in analysing mathematically three kinds of religious belief?

You have to bridge the 'understanding gap' between yourself and the reader. By this stage the researcher is so familiar with the material that it is assumed everyone else is. Bear in mind that the marker of your dissertation may be reading it for the first time and will be considerably irritated if forced to re-read constantly to extract the meaning. The simplest of figures can be obscured by confusing presentation.

Readers need a recognisable conceptual reference. It is hard to visualise 127 out of 246. Percentages have a perennial appeal but can look silly if the sample is very small: 'Five doctors were interviewed and 20% had . . . '. It is not just providing attractive visual presentations that achieves this but matching the style of the presentation to the academic level of the dissertation. For example, some readers find pie charts unsuitable for academic work.

You should recognise four basic scales in analysing data, the first two normally being associated with qualitative and the second two with quantitative research:

- **Nominal scales** are naming or categorising scales used for classifying. Whatever codes are used the scale can only be used for counting from such questions as: Are you in full-time employment? yes/no

- **Ordinal scales** place data in some order, the relative positions of people or things. Without specifying the distance between positions, the scale ranks them from, say, the highest to the lowest. A typical ordinal scale would use a code such as: strongly agree 1 to strongly disagree 5. Only a limited range of statistics may be applied and such scales should not really be averaged.

- **Interval scales** have the properties of ordinal scales but the points on the scale are equal. The researcher sets the units and origin of the scale and must be careful not to make too many unsupportable assumptions about the intervals. For example, in recording Intelligence Quotient scores, is someone with an IQ of 100 the same ten points more intelligent than someone with an IQ of 90 as is someone with an IQ of 140 compared with another of IQ 130?

- **Ratio scales** are common in physical sciences as they have equal intervals and an actual zero point. Used for measuring characteristics such as length, time and weight they have higher mathematical and statistical potential than the others but limited relevance to social scientists whose areas of interest involve human behaviour.

All the scales are possible but be consistent in matching types of data to scales and beware of 'manufacturing' statistics to cover up inadequate data collection and analysis. The lure of numbers is very strong. Did you know that the average number of legs per person in Great Britain is 1.997?

Survey methods are particularly prone to data overload. Some students will cheerfully have ten categories on a ten-point scale thereby producing full but totally unhandleable data from one question. When large amounts of reported factual data need to be shown (do they?), for example a table of average salaries over five years, it is essential that tables, scales and keys are crystal clear if the reader is expected to absorb the information.

Care also needs to be taken with averages which should not be developed from scaled data with intervals of different or unknown size, for example, an ordinal scale such as: very satisfied . . . satisfied . . . dissatisfied . . . very dissatisfied.

Sometimes it is possible to compare obtained data with a reference point such as other research or national norms. Such references need to be clearly attributed and distinguished from the researcher's own data.

Visual summaries such as graphs, pie charts and bar charts are useful and attractive, especially in colour, but can lead to overkill. Some of the most effective dissertations use nothing but simple, well-presented tabulated results: some of the worst are long undifferentiated blocks of descriptive and discursive text.

The reader is entitled to some gloss or interpretation of each block of raw data and attention should be drawn to the most significant items presented, for example,

> From Table 2 it may be seen that the highest levels occurred with . . .

> The low response rates in column 4 were probably caused by . . .

> These figures should be treated with caution as . . .

Purely descriptive, qualitative data can be tricky to present and to avoid tedium they need careful editing and presenting in blocks which can be profitably broken up with sub-headings. Some may not require presenting in full and parts can be relegated to the appendices; for example, interview schedules.

It is advisable to create a title for every table, other than 'fig 2.1' or similar, such as: Patient Discharge Rates in Three Wards.

Below and on the following pages are some examples of data summary presentations.

A simple tabular presentation

Table 6.2
Chemical Analysis of Refractory Sample No 5

Component	*Percentage*
Al_2O_3	68
SeO	13.8
ZrO_2	11.6
MgO	7.2

The analysis was carried out using an X-ray fluorescence spectrometer. The higher level of MgO resulted in changed refractoriness which is shown in Table 6.3.

Hightown Magistrates Court
Recorded Numbers of Offences
January 199X–September 199X

Month	*Total Numbers*	*Males*	*Females*
January	22	20	2
February	16	10	6
March	8	8	0
April	27	25	2
May	19	12	7
June	10	8	2
July	5	4	1
August	0*	0*	0*
September	32	20	12

**No courts held during August*

Survey data can be placed in a simple table but rarely with the same ease of interpretation as physical data. There may be a need for extensive explanations near to the displayed figures.

While the figures in the Hightown Magistrates Court table above show that males consistently committed more offences than females (hardly a startling revelation) they show little else. They could form part of a group of tables linked to the hypothesis or specific research question.

It is necessary to define 'Offence': a prosecution resulting in a conviction or reference to a higher court for sentence. Other variables to consider include the ages of the defendants, the classification of the offences and the actual dates of commission. Another required explanation is the reason for the choice of the nine-month period.

Some data respond well to statistical analysis, especially large quantities of test results, extensive census results or comparative studies; other smaller studies or research into social constructs such as creativity and sensitivity may actually be demeaned by a spurious mathematical gloss.

Work satisfaction levels: workers under 35

Score	*Number*
65–69	*
60–64	****
55–59	*****
50–54	******
45–49	*****
40–44	*
35–39	***
30–34	*
25–29	

n = 26 x = 51.2 s = 8.846

Consider these points about the above example:

- Is it visually attractive?
- Is interpretation easy?
- Is the sample big enough?
- Is there a better way of presenting the results?
- What explanations will be necessary?

Views of parents and pupils about the effects of single sex education for girls

Effect	*Fathers*	*Mothers*	*Girls*
Greater opportunities	66%	44%	16.6%
Fewer distractions	73%	44.4%	6.6%
Greater access to science and computing	20%	25.9%	16.6%
Better social skills	33.3%	14.8%	20%
More confidence	46.7%	33.3%	50%
Enhanced academic ethos	93.3%	37%	50%
Better exam results	73.3%	33.3%	66.6%

The rock on which this research may founder is, of course, the convincing identification of the variables. This will not be improved by any amount of calculation.

The listing of variables is sometimes assumed to invest them with respectability. If this is done in any data summaries a clear expansion and justification should precede them (see the table at the bottom of page 70).

No doubt some valuable information is contained here but the student has a vast task of explanation and linking. You should be able to write a critique of both the data collection and its presentation.

Modern computer graphics offer a huge selection of bar charts: horizontal, vertical, coloured, shaded and three-dimensional. While these have a visual impact it must not obscure the data being presented or assume an importance greater than that of the data. The best advice is: do not try to be too clever and make yourself a lot of counterproductive work.

Average number of days absence per employee by year

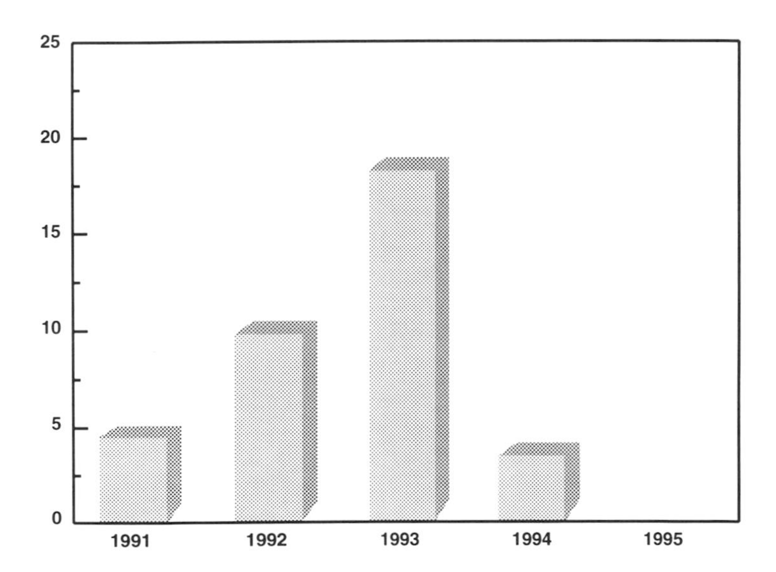

Examine the above example:

- Does the chart make the data clearer?
- What effect does the use of 'average' have on the value of the chart?
- What other numbers or details are necessary?

Number of employees by year since 1989

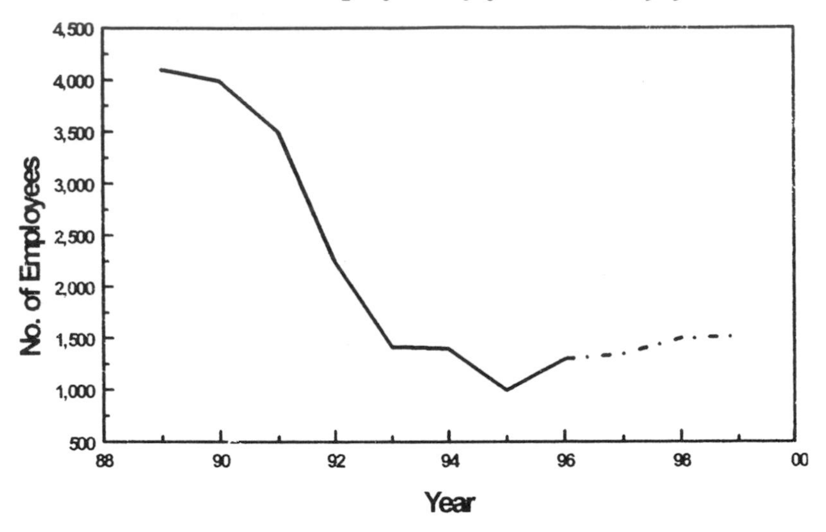

Graphs are a simple and effective visual aid which can be extrapolated to a predicted trend. Care must be taken not to distort either scale to give a false visual impression.

The graph above shows data in support of research into the effects of changes on employment in a large company. Does it display the following three phases in the company development?

1. Re-structuring and introduction of new IT systems.
2. Take-over by another company.
3. Developing new products for EU sales.

What would be the effect of doubling the vertical scale?
What other gloss will be required?

Photographs can be a useful addition to the dissertation, even essential in reporting such data as electron microscopy results, but only if good reproduction can be guaranteed. They do need proper titles, keys and sometimes interpretation.

PRESENTING CONCLUSIONS AND RECOMMENDATIONS

This short but vital section of the dissertation completes the circle begun with the introduction. Results must not be repeated but summarised and related to the hypothesis or research questions. Are they answered, confirmed, nullified? If things have gone wrong how is this explained? Academic integrity demands that you own up to defects and do not attempt any cover-ups.

Remind the reader briefly of what was undertaken and what emerged by way of principal findings or development of theory. Often, the work will suggest further research.

This section, more than any other, is enhanced by concise writing and the use of sub-headings, numbering and bullet points.

Where appropriate—some institutions require it—make practical recommendations arising from your findings and connected to them. Never invent these! For example:

> The findings from the surveys and interviews carried out within the department indicate that changes to the appraisal administration would be welcomed by the staff and bring about greater effectiveness of the system:
>
> 1. issue of preparatory documents one month before the interview
> 2. increase in interview time to one hour
> 3. review of the performance points system.

Rather a neat way to end the section is with another apt quotation, but only if it sounds natural and unforced.

COMPILING THE BIBLIOGRAPHY

This little section can be a crisp hour's work or days of agonised telephoning of libraries and hunting through piles of disorganised paper. It will be a pleasant task only if you have followed the advice about keeping full, accurate, clear and accessible records of all reading of every description.

The bibliography (still often called references in some scientific work) is an ordered list of all the literature used, consulted or quoted from, in a traceable form. The convention is for it to be placed at the end of the main text and before any appendices.

The most important rule is that all literature cited in the text must be identified easily by the reader from the bibliography in a form that makes its acquisition possible.

There are several conventions covering the layout of the bibliography which have generally been simplified over the last few years. It used to be common to have separate sections for books, periodicals and papers but now one alphabetical list is preferred based on the author's surnames. If a work has joint authors, the first named one is used. If more than one work by the same author is cited they appear in date order and if they were published in the same year suffixes a, b . . . are used. If the literature has an 'originator' rather than an author, for example, Department for Education, use that on the left-hand side.

The recommended method is a slight variant of the Harvard system. The author's surname and date of publication, in brackets, are placed offset to the left of the page. If the book has editors rather than authors add (ed) or (eds) after the final name. In the case of multiple authors the abbreviation *et al*, meaning 'and others', is acceptable after the first name. Nothing else goes on the left.

On the right hand side, in order, place:

1. The title, underlined. Capitalise only the first word and any proper nouns.

2. The edition, if not the first.

3. Place of publication, only if unusual or obscure.

4. Name of the publisher.

Avoid unnecessary clutter and be **absolutely consistent**.

Examples:

Banks O. (1993)	The politics of British feminism 1918–1970 Edward Elgar
Bryman A. & Burgess R. G. (eds) (1994)	Analysing qualitative data Routledge
Miller J. C. (1993)	Statistics for analytical chemistry Prentice Hall

Journals and periodicals are recorded in the same way on the left-hand side. The right-hand side is slightly different, as follows:

1. The title of the article, in inverted commas.
2. The title of the journal underlined.
3. Volume and number.
4. The page numbers; use the abbreviation pp for pages.

Examples:

Rouse P. (1994)	'The recognition of executory contracts' Accounting and Business Research No. 97 Winter 1994 pp. 15–21.
Jones M. R. (1994)	'Going to work on an Apple: factors affecting microcomputer use in business organisations' Information systems journal Vol. 4 No. 4 Oct. 1994 pp. 237–252

You will find people who argue passionately for a different scheme. Check any requirements of your institution and examine your bibliography for:

- accuracy
- clarity
- simplicity
- consistency.

APPENDICES

Firstly, what appendices are not. They are **not** a way of avoiding the institution's rules about numbers of words by piling main text into an appendix. They are **not** a way to pad out a short dissertation with other people's work.

The decision about what to put in an appendix is not always easy. A good general rule is that material in an appendix should be optional reading for the general reader, the loss of which should not affect the main themes and conclusions of the research. Examples of materials that belong in appendices include: interview schedules, questionnaires, transcripts of interviews, documents written by others, long statistical analyses and official forms.

Every appendix must be referred to, however briefly, in the main text: for example:

> Records for 1996 were also examined and a summary of those figures is found in Appendix A.
>
> The original pilot questionnaire (see Appendix C) was rejected because . . .

CHECKLIST

Have you:

- written a draft introduction that expresses clearly the purpose of the research, the research questions or hypotheses, the location and its justification?
- completed the reading, both main and research methods, and written a scholarly literature review which covers the general, theoretical and specific background to the work?
- decided how the data will be presented and analysed and started the process?
- started to organise and prepare the bibliography?
- decided the location of data in main text or appendices?

CASE STUDIES

Paul encounters unexpected difficulties

Paul is pleased with the progress of the writing and starts on the empirical work. Disappointingly, the first two householders refuse to talk to him apparently because they think that he is 'from the council'. He also realises that one part of his sample consists of sheltered housing for old people, which will need explanation. Many people are not at home and the original 20% sample has to be increased. Only one farmer refuses to be interviewed and the others provide fascinating insights into the grants and compensation that they have obtained. Most residents have moved from initial hostility to grudging acceptance of the open-cast scheme. The data analysis will concentrate on four aspects: physical effects, and the perceptions of the mining company, residents and farmers. Not only does the data contradict Paul's expectations but he realises that he is barely scratching the surface of the topic—a possible future thesis?

Alison runs into time problems

Alison's colleagues have completed and returned her questionnaire: a lot of prompting was necessary in some cases (does this have any effect on the validity of the data?). The governors and parents prove to be more problematic. After an abortive attempt at a random postal survey she decides to approach the parents via the Parents' Association, with better results. She is given (negotiated by the head) a small amount of time at the end of a main governors' meeting to obtain information and explain her work. Although the data strays considerably from her schedule, she is able after several hours' analysis to see a pattern of priorities emerging from all three groups which she organises as a series of block charts. She is now several weeks behind time and the next main problem is to link the findings with the research questions and her management recommendations.

6
Writing Up

This should be regarded as a tidying-up section. The bulk of your dissertation will be in its virtually final form and in the correct format; nevertheless do not underestimate the time that is required for mechanical tasks. The dissertation will need proofreading at least twice and you may need to enlist help if you find that you are one of many people who just do not see errors. Some departments allow the submission of a draft copy before the final one but most do not and some, as a matter of policy, will never correct students' work. Ultimately the responsibility is yours. Some common gremlins at this stage include:

- spelling, grammar and punctuation
- incorrect formatting on the computer
- wrong pagination
- missing words or references
- cover errors by the binder.

CHOOSING THE STYLE

Check again the rules of the institution. Some business and scientific dissertations may be required in report form, a style that uses strictly limited paragraphs, sometimes of one sentence, each a numbered sub-section of a main section. In its extreme form it is unsuitable for academic dissertations but many lessons can be learned from it, particularly in the value of conciseness, absence of 'waffle', logical progression and the ease of finding a specific point. All dissertations benefit from headed chapters and sections and one style that is definitely not accepted is rambling, discursive and structureless.

Using a detached and passive style

The general academic style used all over the world is detached and passive. Unless there is a special reason personal pronouns are to be avoided. Never 'I showed by my research that . . .' but 'The research showed that . . .'. Other expressions used include: 'The author found . . .', 'The writer . . .'. 'It was discovered that . . .'

Compare paragraph (a) with the rewritten (b):

(a)
I soon realised that my sample of householders would be invalid because of the high numbers that were out or at work. I decided to increase my sample to 50% to ensure that I had sufficient respondents to cover all ranges of opinion. I still have doubts about the high numbers of older people that appeared in my sample and intend to investigate this aspect further.

(b)
It was soon realised that the sample of householders would be invalid because of the high numbers that were out or at work. It was decided to increase the sample to 50% to ensure that there would be sufficient respondents to cover all ranges of opinion. Doubts remained about the high numbers of older people that appeared in the sample and it is intended to investigate this aspect further.

It should be clear that only minor stylistic changes are possible without dramatically increasing the total writing time.

What determines style

Most aspects of style are determined by register (type of audience) and by convention. Even a sophisticated audience finds excessively long sentences difficult to absorb which is probably why the report style evolved. How long? You should be wary of sentences longer than 30 words. Variety is also important.

The tone should be formal and never chatty or frivolous. Written English is not the same as spoken English. All spoken abbreviations should be written in full; no can't, isn't, don't . . . All technical abbreviations and acronyms should be explained at the first time of use.

Tightening up your work

It is too late at this stage to undertake any major revisions in style but you must have had at least one eye on your work to make sure that you are communicating effectively without padding or ambiguity. Could you express the following paragraph in 18 words?

> At this point in time, hopefully, the interviews will indicate a possible mode of procedure for facilitating a revised course of action in the design of questionnaires. Considerations have been given to potential deleterious effects of a sample which is smaller in magnitude than that originally envisaged. While this factor is acknowledged it is superseded by expediency.

CHECKING SPELLING, GRAMMAR AND PUNCTUATION

This is the embarrassing part; skip it if you cannot face it. This taboo subject is rarely mentioned in research methods books but can cause much grief. A hugely frustrating possibility is that the dissertation is passed but that the award is withheld 'Subject to the submission of a corrected copy'. In ten years I have not seen a completely error-free dissertation.

Almost all theses at master's level or above are either lodged in a library or made available for public scrutiny, therefore institutions must be strict about standards.

It was thought, wrongly, that the availability of the spell-checker on computers meant the arrival of a new standard of accuracy in dissertation writing. Strangely, it does not seem to have made much difference. Witness the following passage from a recent Office for Standards in Education report on the teaching of English!

There are inconsistent in standards throughout the key stage particularly in spelling and handwriting.

The standard in speaking and listening skills are good.

In Key stage 2 a range of teachers, parents and other visitors are involved in the development of reading.

The top 20 mistakes

I analysed a wide range of student assignments in response to claims that standards of English were low. Standards were, in fact, quite high but the same band of errors recurred over and over again. Some students were able to eliminate their main errors immediately they were pointed out, even when they had been making the same errors for over 20 years.

The top 20 mistakes included misuse of the apostrophe (well in the lead), the writing of *it's* for the possessive pronoun *its* (easy to correct as the former should never appear in a dissertation); confusion of *principal* (main or head) and *principle* (origin or general law) and crucial misspellings of *questionnaire, liaison, management, consensus, accommodate, benefited, marketing, comparative, comparison, analysis, quantitative, qualitative, definite, professional, committee, commitment, philosophy, psychology, phenomenon* (singular), *phenomena* (plural). More complex words like *homogeneity* seem to present no problem.

Avoiding some common problems

Some very common spellings in dissertations depend on where the **stress** falls in a word. *Benefited* and *marketing* in the list above illustrate this: with the stress on the first syllable the consonant is not doubled before 'ed' or 'ing'. Words that do not follow the rule seem fairly obvious, eg *computing*, *travelling*; the latter being spelled *traveling* in American English.

If the stress falls anywhere else the consonant is more often doubled, eg *professed*, *assessing*. Many other word endings also respond to the same rule. Which of the following spellings is correct: *budgetting* or *budgeting*, *occuring* or *occurring*?

Two words that change their spelling with grammatical function are often seen confused in students' work: *advice* (noun) and *advise* (verb); *practice* (noun) and *practise* (verb). Less commonly, *prophecy* (noun), *prophesy* (verb) and *device* (noun), *devise* (verb) are traps for those who rely too much on spell-checkers. American English is even more confusing on this point.

Careful **pronunciation** will help you to distinguish between words that almost sound alike, such as *compliment* (praise) and *complement* (fill, add). *Definite* also features in the first division of errors.

If you worry that your spelling is really awful you are almost certainly referring to a comparatively small number of recurring errors. I have seen the word *management* misspelled over forty times in one dissertation!

American spellings

American spellings are not all simplified and most spell-checkers are American. Some ruin what few reliable rules we have. The battle for the English spelling of *adviser* has almost been lost, but if you use the American version at least be consistent throughout the dissertation. Scientists have surrendered on *sulfur, fetus* and many others. Try to avoid the more ugly Americanisms such as *hospitalization* and *transportation.* Make a consistent policy decision whether to use s or z in words like *organisation.*

Using the apostrophe

The apostrophe is a special problem. If your work is splattered with them like demented tadpoles try the following basic revision notes:

- The apostrophe is used to show possession or belonging: the manager's work.
- It never appears on ordinary plurals: six managers were interviewed.
- It should not be used on inanimate objects: the closure of the hospital, not the hospital's closure.
- It can always be replaced by 'of the': the work of the manager.

Three basic rules:

1. To show possession on a singular noun, add 's: one nurse's duties included . . .

2. To show possession on a plural noun, add just ': six senior executives' programmes were analysed.

3. To show possession on a plural noun not ending in s, add 's: the children's replies . . .

There are one or two minor complications and exceptions which will probably not be relevant to your dissertation such as days, months and years: one day's work, two years' research, July's results; and on people's names that end in s: Bill Jones' book. What could be easier?

Using simpler punctuation

Punctuation is tending towards simplification. It is now common to see entire letter headings without punctuation of any description and some publishers frown on the colon and semicolon. The latter is unfortunate as these punctuation marks have definite uses which cannot always be replaced by full stops.

Each has two basic uses:

- **Colon**: to introduce a list of objects or ideas as above, or to join two clauses of equal importance but linked in theme. For example:

  Despite close experimental control many of the samples became contaminated with sulphides: it proved extremely difficult to control this contamination.

- **Semicolon**: to separate long and complicated items in a list. For example:

  The sample chosen included various categories: residents who moved into the area within the last year; old established families of several generations; farmers, mostly arable, and occupants of sheltered housing.

  Or to join balanced, connected clauses for the purpose of emphasis:

  The response to the postal surveys was very low; in one case only 4%.

Only use these two endangered species of punctuation marks if they add clarity and variety to the ideas being communicated. You may especially need them if your work is full of sentences beginning with the word 'This'.

Too late for grammar lessons now but if you can become aware of your weaknesses some little tricks may help. Swallow your pride and ask someone! For instance, if you know that you habitually confuse 'there' and 'their' try fitting 'here' into the same space: if it makes some sort of sense, 'there' is the one to use, if not, use the other one. Try it on the following sentence:

> There were many ambiguities in the survey and many respondents confused their replies.

A very common error in students' work (note that apostrophe!) is failure to get the subject of the sentence to agree with the verb, as in the following:

> The group, who had made the greatest number of protests, were not prepared to participate.

If you constantly type the same words wrongly, some word processing software has the auto-correct facility which will operate every time the word is typed. Be careful with this one.

KEEPING A COHERENT THREAD

If the earlier advice was followed the research questions should be engraved on your memory and their progress should be checked throughout every chapter. It is surprisingly easy to lose track of the central thread, especially in the literature review. If it is found that the thread has been lost anywhere edit the text and introduce, where appropriate, short 'reminder' paragraphs where the research questions are referred to directly, keeping the links in a chain which starts at the introduction and ends or completes the circle at the conclusions.

Scrutinise the research methods chapter and check that the justification for the chosen method includes a rationale saying why that method is linked to the problem being researched.

Finally, read the conclusions several times and check that all are intimately connected with the results and that a reader could immediately see whether the hypothesis had been proved or disproved, the questions answered or not, the work evaluated.

PRESENTATION, PRINTING AND BINDING

All awarding institutions have rules about this. Clear copies are essential, ideally laser printed but other good quality ones are acceptable.

Simple spiral binding is common for many first degree projects, usually available at the institution library or visual aids centre for a few pounds. Higher level theses are professionally bound in hard covers with gold lettering. Costs of this vary greatly from area to area; at the time of writing between £15 and 30.

Do not assume the product will automatically be correct. If you give in rubbish to the printer and binder it will emerge as rubbish! Time to redeem disasters must be allowed. Book your binding as soon as you are sure that you are going to submit. The process may take between two days and three weeks. The binder will not fiddle about rearranging things or shuffling papers so do make sure that the dissertation is in its exact, final, proofread form.

Producing the covers

Guidance is usually given about wording on covers; if not, use the following:

- front cover—top centre, title of the dissertation and the name of the author
- front cover—bottom left-hand corner, the qualification, eg BSc
- front cover—bottom right-hand corner, the year of submission
- spine—author's surname, abbreviated title, qualification and year.

Inside the covers, the correct order is as follows:

- title page
- contents page

A Typical Cover

THE INTRODUCTION AND MANAGEMENT OF AN APPRAISAL SYSTEM IN A SMALL INDUSTRIAL PLANT

P S. BARLOW

MSc 1996

SPINE

BARLOW	APPRAISAL MANAGEMENT	MSc 1996

- acknowledgements (if any)
- preface (if any)
- body of the text
- bibliography
- appendices.

Abstracts

You may be required to include an **abstract** bound in before the body of the text or to provide one separately. Abstracts are very brief outline summaries of the purpose of the work and its main findings.

It is customary to acknowledge the help of a tutor or supervisor and any special assistance by outsiders. Acknowledgements should be brief and never fulsome; for example:

> The author acknowledges the assistance of Dr P. Gold and the provision of documents by the Physiology Department of Hightown Hospital.

Proofreading

Proofreading your own work is a long, tedious task which gets worse as the student becomes more and more familiar with it. Very few people can proofread for meaning and technicalities at the same time. Do you need help? Test your abilities on the following passage which must be done in 30 seconds:

> Research was focused on the activities of the liesure center over a period of six months and exellent cooperation was recieved from all staff who participated in the the study. A group of users were followed throughout the research and questionaires were collected from them at theend of the project, other seperate groups sessions, such as evening only users, were asked informerly about there views on the range of facilitys in which they were particulary interested.

At least 17 errors are present.

A possible corrected version

> Research was focused on the activities of the leisure centre over a period of six months and excellent co-operation was received from all staff who participated in the study.

> A group of users was followed throughout the research and questionnaires were collected from them at the end of the project. Other separate groups' sessions, such as evening only users, were asked informally about their views on the range of facilities in which they were particularly interested.

There are, of course, other questions that could be raised about style.

CHECKLIST

Have you:

- checked that a consistent theme runs through the whole dissertation?
- followed the house rules of the institution?
- put everything in the correct order and format?
- done the final editing?
- proofread the entire work?
- booked a binder?

CASE STUDIES

Paul has to make cuts

Paul has now virtually finished but realises that the work will run to at least 12,000 words. He requests permission to exceed the total; the tutor refuses. He is rather held up by the breakdown of the colour photocopier, the need to rewrite part of the research methods section and the discovery of two missing references in the literature review. What can be edited out? He decides on several pages of interview transcriptions, part of the introduction which is repeated in the literature review and two pages of research methods which cover styles that were not used.

Alison needs to rewrite

Alison has caught up a little but resolves to devote a complete week of the Easter holidays to analysis and writing up the empirical work. She feels that there are some really valuable answers to research questions one, two and four but the data on three are very thin. There is no chance of any further empirical work and she decides to risk it with an explanatory paragraph in the conclusions. Her tutor advises that her management recommendations need closer identification with the actual data found—two pages to rewrite. She is glad that she followed advice about initial planning as she can see the total pattern of the dissertation.

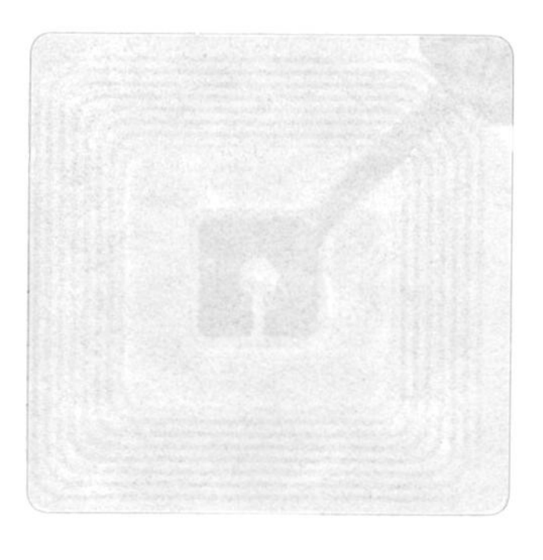

7
The Final Stage

MARK YOUR OWN DISSERTATION

Well, not really, but it is a useful exercise as part of the final editing to assess your own work in the way that the university or college will do. Use the following criteria to evaluate the research report:

Introduction

- Is there a clear outline of the purpose of the work, the hypothesis or research questions?
- Is there a justification of the origin and likely value of the research?
- Is its locus and context made clear?
  Allocate marks up to a maximum of five.

Literature review

- Does the literature thoroughly underpin the theory relating to the study?
- Is it wide ranging from the general to the specific, books and journals?
- Is the work of others acknowledged and glossed?
- Is there constant relation to your objectives?
- Is there pertinent and relevant use of quotation?
  Allocate marks up to a maximum of 25.

Research methodology

- Is there a critical review of possible methodologies?
- Is a convincing rationale evident for the style and approach to be used?
- Are possible techniques for data collection proposed?
- Is a population and sample outlined?
  Allocate a maximum of ten marks.

Data collection and analysis

- Is it clear that the data were collected systematically and logically by appropriate methods?
- Is there convincing interpretation and inference linked to the data presented?
- Have issues of reliability, validity and generalisability been considered?
- Are instruments, scales and statistics relevant and effective?
  Allocate a maximum of 25 marks.

Conclusions and recommendations

- Do the conclusions follow logically from the data presented?
- Do they maintain a clear link with the initially stated objectives of the research?
- Are they a scholarly and fair assessment of the results?
- Are the recommendations convincing and practical?
  Allocate a maximum of 15 marks.

Structure and presentation

- Are the sections and chapters balanced and well structured?
- Is there a high standard of spelling, grammar and punctuation?

- Are all references consistent, accurate and reflected in a good bibliography?
  Allocate a maximum of ten marks.

Overall impression

- Is there a definite coherence in the finished product?

- Does the study make a satisfying contribution to understanding, knowledge and practice?
  Allocate a maximum of ten marks.

Other criteria that may be applied, depending on the type of study, include: quality of experimental work, accuracy and relevance of statistics and appropriate ethical considerations.

Remember that you do not need 100% to pass; 40–45% is a more usual target which may be for each section rather than overall. If the student has worked conscientiously and fulfilled the requirements, it is more difficult to fail than pass!

Practices in awarding institutions vary greatly. Some make their criteria explicit, others do not. Some allow looser structures or pay more attention to overall impression. Occasionally students despair of ever getting any information of any description and are left to blunder along.

Very few postgraduate qualifications are classified but are awarded on a pass/fail basis. A few universities, notably in Scotland, award masters' degrees 'with distinction'. At lower levels the marks for the research project will be subsumed into the total marks, often with a proviso that it must be passed.

PREPARING FOR A VIVA

Just when you thought it was safe to forget everything this emerges! A viva (*viva voce*) is an oral examination on your research work and its results conducted either by internal or external tutors and lasting about 15 to 30 minutes. It needs a plan, just like everything else in the dissertation. Generally a formal mark is not given but it is used to supplement parts of the dissertation and to explore the student's depth of understanding. A second function is for the external examiner to moderate the work of the tutorial staff so you could be asked questions about your work on other parts of the course. If this happens, be a constructive 'critical friend' and do not carp.

Practice again varies widely: at first degree level all students may be examined; elsewhere, a sample is taken. The student may be selected for a number of reasons:

- the work is brilliant
- it is a failure
- it is borderline
- it is a random sample.

As the student is unlikely to find out which, it is unproductive to worry unnecessarily but essential to prepare thoroughly. The examiner is inevitably on your side and is as helpful as possible. On the day, look smart and be friendly without being gushing. The examiner will expect you to develop answers from his or her direct leads.

In preparation the dissertation *must* be read again and notes made on any perceived inadequacies or omissions. Typical questions to expect include:

- What aspects of the research caused you the greatest difficulty?
- Were you satisfied with the method and sample?
- Could you say a little more about . . . ?
- What did you personally gain from the work?
- How could this research be developed further?
- Which conclusion do you see as the most significant?

None of these can be answered without confident knowledge of the dissertation.

WHAT HAPPENS NOW?

Check the printed and bound copy for the last time and give it in, if possible at least a fortnight before the deadline. Keep at least one copy and download everything from the computer onto a floppy disk. Ask when results will be available, usually between a month and six weeks.

The dissertation will be marked by the department controlling

the subject, commonly by two tutors, perhaps by three or more if there is controversy. If any validated qualification is to be awarded the provisional results are submitted to an Examination Board, which is headed by an external academic whose duty is to ensure that national standards are maintained and moderated and to arbitrate in disputes.

Several results are possible:

- pass (the most likely one)
- fail (very rare)
- fail due to non-submission (quite common)
- deferred (some problem such as an unacceptable copy)
- referred (a breach of regulations)
- aegrotat (problems with illness).

The organisation may be prepared to give results by telephone at an appointed time but do not pester them; they have hundreds of anxious students to deal with. All results are posted on a notice board on a pre-arranged day.

Relax and wait.

REPAIRING A DISASTER

You will probably realise well before the submission date whether the dissertation reaches the acceptable standard and if it does not the cause is likely to rest with your commitment and motivation, especially in the case of non-submission. Other reasons are possible such as family problems and illness. If possible you should confide in a tutor, and in the event of illness medical certificates are essential for appeals for special consideration or extension of time. If any appeal is undertaken on procedural or academic grounds precise documentary evidence should be submitted to the Examination Board well before the meeting. This course of action is only to be undertaken in wholly exceptional situations.

If an opportunity is given to re-submit or to continue for another year do not be tempted to take a break or the impetus will be lost. Take tutorial advice and start to resurrect the project; it may only need minor adjustments. Do not, despite your disappointment, give up at the last hurdle.

CHECKLIST

Have you:

- assessed your own dissertation?
- double-checked final submission date, time and place?
- delivered to the binder and secured a firm collection date?
- cleared the date for the viva and prepared for it if required?
- written the abstract, if separate?

CASE STUDIES

Paul underestimates himself

Paul solved his remaining problems and edited the work down to 10,500 words which was accepted. The missing references were never found and two useful quotations had to be eliminated from the literature review. He can see the defects in the work but is basically pleased with the product. His self-assessment of the dissertation suggests a mark of 60%. It is spiral bound by the university library at a cost of £2.50 and is submitted to the geography department a week before the deadline. In fact it scores 70% and helps considerably towards his final degree classification of 2:1.

Alison impresses the examiner

Alison's sacrifice of holiday has achieved the desired effect and all writing has been completed. When she proofreads the text she realises that this success has given the latter part of the dissertation a rather rushed tone. Her self-assessment comes to 40%. She is cheered up by the attractive appearance of the dissertation when it returns from the binder (£25) and gives it in with one day to spare. Called for a viva she prepares extensively and, sure enough, the examiner asks her about the 'lost' research question and is impressed by her convincing justification. She is awarded the degree of MA (Educational Studies) and resolves to spend more time with her family!

Further Reading

Doing Your Research Project Bell J. (Open University 1989). A popular, general guide.

Analysing Qualitative Data Bryman & Burgess (eds) (Routledge 1994). Specific techniques.

Quantitative Data Analysis for Social Scientists Bryman & Cramer (Routledge 1994). Revised, updated, some computer.

Research Methods in Education Cohen & Manion (Routledge 1989). A standard work.

Statistics for Social Scientists Cohen L. & Holliday M. (PCP Ltd 1982). Basic concepts, very clear, some computer programs.

Research Methods and Statistics in Psychology Coolican H. (Hodder & Stoughton 1990). Specialist psychology.

Research Methods in Physical Activity (2nd ed) Thomas & Nelson (Champaign Ill. 1990). Specialist sports science.

Handbook of Qualitative Research Denzin & Lincolm (eds) (Sage Publications 1994). Long, complex, American book, very expensive; to be dipped into.

How to Design and Evaluate Research in Education (2nd ed) Fraenkel & Wallen (McGraw Hill Inc 1993). Expensive, American but excellent, useful for all social sciences.

Planning a Research Project Herbert M. (Cassell 1990). Health & caring professions.

Doing Research in Sensitive Areas Lee R. (Sage Publications 1993). Sociology, specialist techniques.

Foundations of Experimental Research (3rd ed) Plutchik R. (Harper & Row NY 1983). Basic psychological experiments.

Interviewing in Educational Research Powney & Watts (Routledge & Kegan Paul 1987). Very specific techniques.

Real World Research Robson C. (Blackwell 1993). General social sciences, excellent basics.

Survey Research: a Decisional Approach Tull & Albaum (Intertext Books 1973). Basic statistical approach.
Surveys in Social Research de Vaus D. (3rd ed) (UCL Press 1993). Standard text.

Physical scientists are well served by texts that tend to be very specific to a discipline and also to concentrate on techniques, such as:

Ecological Experiments, Purpose, Design and Execution Hairston N. G. (Cambridge 1989).
Statistics for Analytical Chemistry Miller J. C. (Prentice Hall 1993).
Geographical Data-Sources, Presentation and Analysis Matthews & Foster (Oxford University Press 1989).

Glossary

Abstract A brief written summary of the purpose, results and conclusions of your research, usually submitted separately from the dissertation.

Action research Where the researcher is involved in a situation, makes changes and observes the effects.

Bibliography An ordered list of works consulted or referred to in the dissertation.

Case study Research into one particular group or defined institution, describing and investigating the variables and relationships.

Correlational research Exploring the possible relationships between variables.

Convenience sample A sample chosen because it is easily available.

Data All the information and facts collected from your samples.

Dependent variable A variable which takes on values when an independent variable is deliberately altered.

Descriptive research Describing what exists in your sample in a structured way without analysing variables.

Empirical Based on observation, experiment and recording.

Epistemology The philosophy of knowledge and ways of knowing.

Ethics Philosophical systems of belief and values.

Ethnography Study of a group's culture, customs and behaviour by observation and recording.

Ethnomethodology Very specialised qualitative research into patterns of human talk, communication and meaning.

Experiment Obtaining data by quantitative methods with scientific precision and control.

Generalisability (external validity) Can your results be applied or be useful to others?

Historical research Structured study of past events to help with current problems or understanding.

Hypothesis A tentative or supposed proposition based on observed happenings or theories about a testable relationship or quality.

Idiographic Private, personal, individual characteristics.

Independent variable The variable controlled by the researcher to investigate its effects on others.

Instrument Any research 'tool' such as a questionnaire used to obtain data.

Interpretative Subjective explaining and interpreting of data.

Interval scale A scale where test and measurement results have supposedly equal intervals.

Nominal scale Scales designed to label or categorise groups and their qualities.

Ordinal scale Ranking people according to how much they possess a given quality.

Positivist Considering only observable, objective facts.

Purposive sample A non-random sample of those believed to be representative.

Qualitative Concerned with description, qualities and observation.

Quantitative Concerned with measurement and numbers.

Questionnaire A structured set of written questions designed to obtain information from a sample.

Random sample Where every member of a population has an equal chance of being selected.

Ratio scale A scale that has intervals and an absolute zero.

Reliability Would you get the same results if you repeated the procedure?

Research question A proposed focus of inquiry; what you want to find out.

Sample A group selected from a studied population which supposedly possesses the same characteristics as the whole.

Semi-structured A schedule for interviews which has a partially planned framework.

Structured A completely planned framework of interview questions.

Stratified sample A sample selected to represent an identifiable group in the same proportion as it exists in the total population.

Survey A method of obtaining data about variables from a population or a sample of it.

Systematic sample A sample taken at equal, regular intervals, eg every tenth name on a register.

Validity How far you are actually measuring the variable that you say you are measuring.

Viva (*viva voce*) An oral examination on research work and its results conducted either by internal or external tutors and lasting about 15 to 30 minutes.

Index